ECOTOURISM AND LIVELIHOODS

By the same author

Community Participation and Sustainable Forest Development: Global Perspective

---

About the Editor

A.K. Bhattacharya is an Indian Forest Service officer of 1983 batch from Madhya Pradesh cadre. He is presently an Associate Professor and Conservator of Forests in Indian Institute of Forest Management, Bhopal, an autonomous organisation under the Ministry of Environment and Forests, Government of India.

Dr. Bhattacharya is Post Doctoral in Environmental Sciences and has contributed a large number of articles in national and international journals on a range of topics related to forestry and environment. Also, he has to his credit a book on 'Kandhar Plane Hijack', based on his own experience as a hostage.

His main contributions to the field of eco-tourism include organising capacity building workshops and training courses for the local authorities of various concerned departments, communities and NGOs, extending professional support to the State Government for promotion of eco-tourism, supervising research works on eco-tourism related topics, and preparing Eco-tourism Management Plans for few protected areas.

ECOTOURISM
AND
LIVELIHOODS

Capacity Building for Local Authorities

A.K. Bhattacharya, *IFS*
Indian Institute of Forest Management
Bhopal (M.P.), India

CONCEPT PUBLISHING COMPANY, NEW DELHI-110059

ISBN: 978-81-8069-174-4

Edition 2026

Published and Printed by

Concept
Since 1974

Concept Publishing Company Pvt. Ltd.
A/15-16, Commercial Block, Mohan Garden
New Delhi-110059 (India)
T: +91-11-41101460
E: publishing@conceptpub.com, *W*: www.conceptpub.com

Cataloging in Publication--Courtesy: D.K. Agencies (P) Ltd. <docinfo@dkagencies.com>

Ecotourism and livelihoods : capacity building for local authorities / [edited by] A.K. Bhattacharya.
P. cm.
Papers presented at various workshops and training courses.
Includes bibliographical references.
Includes index.
ISBN 8180691748

1. Ecotourism. 2. Ecotourism—India—Madhya Pradesh. I. Bhattacharya, A.K.

DDC 338.479 1543 21

N.K. JOSHI

वन महानिदेशक एवं विशेष सचिव
भारत सरकार
पर्यावरण एवं वन मंत्रालय
DIRECTOR GENERAL OF FORESTS
& SPL. SECY.
GOVERNMENT OF INDIA
MINISTRY OF ENVIRONMENT & FORESTS

सत्यमेव जयते

Tel No. 2436 1509
Fax No. 2436 3957
e-mail: nkjoshi_moenf@yahoo.com

FOREWORD

Tourism is the fastest growing industry in the world, and as a result is also a large scale activity of global human society, with its negative impacts on the natural environment.

Ecotourism, as a specialized form of tourism, has been found to provide a new dimension to the tourism industry by reducing these impacts. Ecotourism has potential to improve sustainability by modifying various components with regard to the conservation of the natural resources. Thus ecotourism can prove to be a very effective tool for the sustainability of the ecosystem and at the same time positively contribute to the community development.

In order to achieve the goals of the sustainable ecotourism the capacity building of the various stakeholders is an essential and challenging task. Indian Institute of Forest Management, Bhopal has taken up ecotourism as an area of specialization for training and research. Over the last few years the Institute has made constant efforts in this direction for the orientation and capacity building of various stakeholders to use ecotourism as an effective tool for sustainable forest development. The author has successfully conducted a series of Workshops and Training Courses for the capacity building of the local authorities and also undertaken many research projects on ecotourism. The book is a good effort to compile the outcome of these studies and Workshops and Training Courses. The inclusion of on-field experience of the author and the experience of various stakeholders are the value addition to the book. The book will prove to be very useful for all the practitioners, researchers and other stakeholders in planning and implementation of ecotourism.

(N.K. Joshi)

BARKATULLAH UNIVERSITY, BHOPAL (M.P.)

Dr. Ram Prasad, *IFS*
VICE CHANCELLOR &
PRINCIPAL CHIEF CONSERVATOR
OF FORESTS, MADHYA PRADESH

Ph. (O) : 0755-2587236, 5290671
(R) : 0755-2424907
Fax : (91) 0755-2581835

FOREWORD

The year 2002 was celebrated as International Year of Ecotourism. This signifies the relevance and recognition of ecotourism both locally and globally. The lessons learned in 2002 should reach beyond the International Year of Ecotourism in time, space and range of travel niches. For the benefits of ecotourism to be relevant locally and globally it is required to change the way tourism operates today. For this, one of the essential efforts that should be made is the capacity building of all stakeholders who can understand and implement ecotourism in a way that it contributes actively to the conservation of knowledge and cultural heritage and development of the indigenous communities. In order to minimise the negative impacts of tourism and maximise the community benefits, the training of the tourism managers is essential to orient them for the sustainable ecotourism.

Dr.A.K. Bhattacharya of Indian Institute of Forest Management, Bhopal has constantly made efforts in this direction to orient and build up the capacities of the managers and local authorities to use ecotourism as an effective tool for sustainable forest development. The author has conducted a series of Workshops and Training Courses for the capacity building of the local authorities and also undertaken many research projects on ecotourism. The book is an outcome of these studies and Workshops and Training Courses and contains on-field experience of the author and the experience of various stakeholders. The book will be very useful for the practitioners, local authorities, academicians and researchers in planning and implementation of ecotourism. I congratulate the author of this book and look forward to continue his campaign for sustainable ecotourism.

(Dr RAM PRASAD)

A.P. DWIVEDI *I.F.S.*
PRINCIPAL CHIEF CONSERVATOR
OF FORESTS, MADHYA PRADESH

O/o Principal Chief
Conservator of Forests
Madhya Pradesh,
Satpura Bhawan,
Bhopal

FOREWORD

Tourism today is the world's largest growing civilian industry with no signs of slowing down in the twenty-first century. This sector has a multiplier effect, for every rupee invested in building the infrastructure the revenue generated is more than three times. Consequently, the tourism, if not planned and managed properly and scientifically, has far reaching consequences on the physical and cultural environments of the tourism destination areas. As an ideal principle, tourism should be developed within the carrying capacity of the natural resources of the tourism destination areas so as to preserve the environment. The last decade has witnessed the emergence of a paradigm of sustainable tourism development one which appears to adopt a responsible course balancing the requirements of tourism development with the conservation of environment.

Ecotourism is a sustainable path to tourism development and is being promoted as a means of giving nature a value and hence of achieving sustainable tourism. The objective of ecotourism is to promote sustainable tourism, which involves overall development of the local community and a better understanding and appreciation of natural and cultural features of the host population leading to international, interregional and intercultural understanding for sustainable development.

The involvement of the local communities and other stakeholders is an important component to achieve the goals of ecotourism, and for this, one of the significant tasks is the capacity building of all stakeholders for their proper orientation and skill development. Indian Institute of Forest Management, Bhopal has made fruitful efforts for capacity building training and research in the area of ecotourism. The author has made constant efforts over the last few years for the orientation and capacity building of various stakeholders to use ecotourism as an effective tool for sustainable forest development. The author has successfully conducted a series of

Workshops and Training Courses for the capacity building of the local authorities and also undertaken many research projects on ecotourism. The book is an excellent compilation of the outcome of the research projects undertaken by the author and the Workshops and Training Courses. The reflections of the field experience of the author and the experience of various stakeholders are the significant contributions of the book. The book should prove to be very useful to provide useful information, future research road map and guidelines for all the practitioners, researchers and other stakeholders for effective planning and implementation of sustainable ecotourism.

(A.P. Dwivedi)
PCCF & Chief Wildlife Warden, MP

ACKNOWLEDGEMENTS

The author acknowledges the assistance and inputs of the researchers, Mr. Thriveen Sankar and Sumeet Matta, in the finalisation of the manuscript.

CONTENTS

THE CONTRIBUTORS

Bala, Sanjay, PPCCF, M.P. Forest Department.

Banerjee, Suchitra, Department Zoology, M.L.B. College, Bhopal, (M.P.)

Bhattacharya, A.K., Associate Professor, Indian Institutes of Forest Management, Bhopal.

Bijendra Basuyat, Assistant Professor, Indian Institute of Forest Management Bhopal.

Dubey, Yogesh, Assistant Professor, Indian Institute of Forest Management Bhopal.

Ghosh, Sudipto, PPCCF, M.P. Forest Department.

Kumar Rahul, PPCCF, M.P. Forest Department.

Pabla, H.S., PPCCF, M.P. Forest Department.

Rathore, B.M.S., PPCCF, M.P. Forest Department.

Saksena, Vandana, Researcher, Centre for Environment Sciences, Jiwaji University, Gwalior, M.P.

Sankar, Thriveen, Researcher, Centre for Environment Sciences, Jiwaji University, Gwalior, M.P.

Saxena, Alark, PPCCF, M.P. Forest Department.

1

INTRODUCTION

A.K. Bhattacharya

Ecotourism

The term ecotourism was coined by Hector Ceballos Lascurian in 1983. The term was used to describe the nature-based travel with emphasis on education, management and development of sustainable tourism product and activity.

Definition for Ecotourism

World Tourism Organisation has defined ecotourism as "tourism that involves travelling to relatively undisturbed natural areas with specified object of studying, admiring and enjoying the scenery and its wild plants and animals, as well as any existing cultural aspects (both of past and present) found in these areas".

The Ecotourism Society (TES) defined Ecotourism as "responsible travel to natural areas that conserves the environment and sustains the well-being of the local people". Its main aims are ecological and socio-cultural integrity, responsibility and sustainability (Cater, 1994). Ecotourism has developed from the traditional nature tourism and sustainable development concepts.

Other Standard Definitions of Ecotourism

Ecotourism has been defined differently by different experts in their perspective, although all the definitions have certain common components. All the standard definitions have been examined to capture different dimensions of ecotourism.

Purposeful travel to natural areas to understand the culture and history of the environment, taking care not to alter the integrity of the eco-system, while producing economic opportunities that make conservation of natural resources beneficial to local people.

—RECOFTC, FAO

Responsible travel to natural areas that conserves the environment and sustains the well-being of local people.

—Epler Wood, 1996
The Eco-Tourism Society (TES)
Sources: RECOFTC

Eco-tourism is defined as travel to wilderness areas for admiring and enjoying the bio-diversity and cultural heritage.

—WII
Source: Workshop on Wildlife Tourism Management in India, WII

Eco-tourism is not mass-tourism behind green marks. Eco-tourism means a constant struggle to defend the earth and to protest and sustain traditional communities. "Eco-tourism is a co-operative relationship between the non-wealthy local community and those open-minded tourists who went to enjoy themselves in a third world outing".

—Talemeca Association of Eco-Tourism and Conservation in Cota Ricd.

Eco-tourism is based on appreciation of and consideration for the natural and cultural environment.

—Bridger

Community Tourism

Tourism in which local residents (often rural, often poor and marginalized) are active participants as land managers, entrepreneurs employer, decision makers and conservators. It is not just a community co-operative running company. The aim is for residents to say in decisions over tourism development in their areas and mark with other stakeholders to develop opportunities for employment enterprise, skill development, and other improvements in local livelihoods.

—Africa Resource Trust, IUCN, WWF, USAID, SADC.

We are trying to help the local communities in our foul area devise and publicise volunteer options. The advantages of this scenario should be clear: The village gets free help and revenue from the tourist: the tourist gets the experience of a lifetime, and probably developer a life-long relationship with the village that will result in return visits and invaluable word of mouth promotion

—Bridger, PRTD

Travelling to undisturbed areas or uncontaminated natural areas with the specific objective of studying, admiring, and enjoying the scenery and its wild plants and animals.

—Ceballar - Vasurain, 1987

A born of tourism inspired primarily by the natural history of an area, including its indigenous cultures. The eco-tourists visit relatively undeveloped areas in the spirit of appreciation, participation, and sensitivity.

—Ziffer, 1989

One of the essential ingredients of eco-tourism is community participation and community benefits.

—Ecotourism workshop

Nature-based tourism that involves education and interpretation of the natural environment and is managed to be ecologically sustainable (Commonwealth Department of Tourism: 1994)

—Env. Auditing and Eco-Tourism: A Case Study

Some experts buy the term originated from Kenton Miller, a pioneer of eco-development and sustainability. In his writing regarding National Park planning in Latin America, Miller argued that—"Development must integrate biological considerations with economic, social and political factors to meet both environmental and human needs."

—Popers

Eco-tourism is "Sustainable, nature tourism" involving the indigenous stakeholders, while forging partnership with the existing tourism industry.

—Eco-Tourism in MP: Policy Guidelines (1999)

In simple words Eco-tourism is sustainable, site specific, people friendly Wildlife Tourism approach where indigenous people's participation is ensured both at planning and implementation levels. In other words Eco-tourism is tourism of the people, for the people and by the people.

—Promotion of Community based Eco-tourism for protected area of M.P.

Hector Ceballos Lascurian has been credited with first using the term in 1983. He defined eco-tourism as "Travelling to relatively undisturbed or uncontaminated natural area with the specific objective of studying, admiring, and enjoying the scenery and its wild plants, as well as any existing cultural manifestations (both past and present) found in these areas.

—Eco-tourism; Discussion paper on Natural based tourism July 1994

The original vision of eco-tourism is that it must be (i) small scale; (ii) locally controlled and ecologically sensitive and that it must fulfil the following criteria, i.e., it must be—

(i) Environmentally socially, culturally and economically sustainable
(ii) Educational
(iii) Local participatory

—Papers on Eco-tourism and Conservation Education by Suhas Kumar

"A phenomenon composed of a spectrum of options, ranging from a hand core, scientific approach to visit a natural area as a weekend activity or a part of a broader trip."—Boo (1990): Visits to national parks and other natural areas with the aim of viewing and enjoying the plants and animals as well as any indigenous culture.

—Ecotourism Association of Australia (1992) "Ecologically Sustainable Tourism that fosters environmental and cultural understanding, appreciation and conservation".

—The National Eco-tourism Strategy
[Commonwealth of Australia] (1994)

"Ecotourism is nature based tourism that involves education and interpretation of the natural environment and is managed to be ecologically sustainable".

—Ecotourism Planning and Management
(24th-30th May, 2000)

WTO defines sustainable tourism as—"Sustainable Tourism Development that meets the needs of present tourists and host regions while protecting and enhancing opportunities for the future. It is envisaged as leading to management of all resources in such a way that economic, social and aesthetic needs can be fulfilled while maintaining cultural integrity, essential ecological processes, biological diversity, and life support systems."

—Guide for local Authorities on Developing
Sustainable Tourism

The World Tourism Report defines—Sustainable Tourism as a mode: Form of economic development that exemplifies stewardship of environment and sensitivity to community and cultural aspirations.

A new dimension has been added by sustainable tourism. It takes into account both the conservation and preservation of the physical and cultural environment of a particular region.

—Tourism Management by Akshaya Kumar

The activities of persons travelling to and staying in places outside their usual environment for not more than one consecutive year for leisure, business and other purposes constitute tourism. Such visits for being with nature to enjoy its enormous creations both biotic and abiotic, in a most environment friendly manner without any adverse impact on the eco-system is particularly known as eco-tourism.

—DOSSIER, Eco-Tourism

Sustainable tourism development is envisaged as leading to management of all resources in such a way that we can fulfil economic, social and aesthetic needs while maintaining cultural integrity, essential ecological processes, biological diversity and life support systems.

—An Action Strategy for Sustainable
Tourism Development Van Couver,
British Columbia, Canada March, 1990

"Low Impact nature tourism which contributes to the maintenance of species and habitats either directly through a contribution to conservation and / or indirectly by providing revenue to the local community sufficient for people to value and, therefore, protect their wildlife heritage area as a source of income."

—Goodwin, 1996

Ecotourism is a nature based tourism that involves education and interpretation of the natural environment and is managed to be ecologically sustainable.

—National Eco-tourism Strategy, Commonwealth
Dept. of Tourism

Tourism that involves travelling to relatively undisturbed natural area with the specified objective of studying, admiring and enjoying the scenery and its wild plants and animals.

—W.T.O., Natural Area Tourism

Long Term success of sustainable eco-tourism ultimately depends upon community perception and involvement in planning and management of sustainable eco-tourism.

—Craik, 1991

Eco-tourism is tourism that is environmentally sensitive.

—Muloin 1991

An enlightening nature travel experience that contributes to the conservation of the ecosystem while respecting the integrity of host communities.

—Cater and Zowmen, 1994

Principles and Characteristics of Ecotourism

- It should be small scaled, locally controlled, land sensitive and ecologically oriented.
- It should be based on environmental ethics with a concept of 'small is beautiful', doing more with less and treated with fostering resource integrity.
- It should be sustainable environmentally, socially, culturally and economically.
- It should enrich experience and should be educational.
- It should have the participation of the local communities.
- It is bio-centric rather than homocentric in philosophy. In fact ecotourism should accept nature largely on its terms and not trying to significantly transform nature for personal convenience.

Community Based Ecotourism

Humankind is facing an unparalleled challenge when it comes to reserving the planet's biodiversity. Solutions that are most likely to be successful are those that will work at the community level in a decentralized manner. So for the successful efforts in ecotourism promotion, the community or people's participation is vital. Community based ecotourism implies that a community is taking care of their natural resources in order to gain income through operating a tourism enterprise and using that income to better their lives. It is also a better option for the people from the developing countries as an alternate means of livelihood, as it can both protect the resource base if properly managed and can act as an economic source.

People's Participation is essential for Sustainable Tourism because:

- Communities are an integral part of ecotourism ecosystem. They can help sustain ecosystem.
- Communities are to be affected first by any influences of ecotourism destination areas.
- For sustainable tourism, involvement of communities in planning and local management is essential.
- Since ecotourism brings many changes at the community level, therefore, community should have greater voice in development and conservation of their natural resources.

Why Ecotourism?

- Avoids negative impacts that can damage or destroy the integrity or character of the natural or cultural environments being visited.
- Educates the traveller on the importance of conservation.
- Directs revenues to the conservation of natural areas and the management of protected areas.
- Brings economic benefits to local communities and directs revenues to local people living adjacent to protected areas.
- Emphasizes the need for planning and sustainable growth of the tourism industry and seeks to ensure that tourism development does not exceed the social and environmental "carrying capacity".
- Retains a high percentage of revenues in the host country by stressing the use of locally-owned facilities and services.
- Increasingly relies on infrastructure that has been developed sensitively in harmony with the environment—minimizing use of fossil fuels, conserving local plant and wildlife and blending with natural environment.

Capacity Building for the Development of Ecotourism

Capacity building has to be carried out for all the stakeholders. The Forest and Tourism Departments should be given training for the management of ecotourism activities. In this case there should be a proper identification of functions of Forest and Tourism Departments and accordingly required training should be imparted. The capacity building activities can include seminars, workshops, field visits, orientation programmes, etc.

The tourism facility operators should be given the training for management of ecologically attuned facilities and also the best management practices for resorts. They should also be made aware about the different laws and policies for sustainable tourism activities.

The local people should be given the training for dealing with tourists, both from the management level and from host population's point of view. Exposure visits to community based ecotourism centres will be a useful tool for this purpose.

As a part of the efforts for capacity building of different stakeholders of ecotourism, Madhya Pradesh Forest Department, MP Tourism Development Corporation in collabora-tion with IIFM conducted various seminars and workshops, whose summary is given below.

Objectives of Workshops and Training Courses

- Impart education and awareness about importance of different aspects of ecotourism.
- Develop ecotourism as a management tool for natural resource protection and biodiversity conservation.
- Improve livelihood options of local communities through ecotourism activities.
- Expose the participants to practical aspects of ecotourism by field visits and discussion about case studies.

Design of Workshops and Training Courses

The workshops and training courses were designed in the following framework:

- The courses included into theory classes followed by practical sessions through field visits.
- The theory classes included different aspects of ecotourism and livelihood including introduction to ecotourism concepts, community benefits for local people from ecotourism, biodiversity conservation, economic valuation of ecotourism, environmental auditing, livelihood options, etc.
- Experts in these fields participated as resource persons for these classes and participants were encouraged to critically analyse these issues and give suggestions for the same.
- The theory classes also included case studies of successful models of ecotourism to broaden the knowledge sphere of participants to the innovative and upcoming trends in various dimensions of ecotourism.
- The other major part of the capacity building programme was the field exercises undertaken in different ecotourism destination areas with ecotourism potential in and around Bhopal.
- In these field visits, participants were assigned with specific tasks in groups and at the end of the exercise they had to present the results for further discussions.

Pattern for Workshops and Training Courses

Theory Classes

- Lectures by resource persons
- Case Studies
- Panel discussion
- Feedback and Recommendations

Feedback and Field Exercises

- Tourists' perception
- Villagers' perception
- Perspective plan formulation for an ecotourism destination area
- Presentation of results

Topics of Discussion

Following major topics were discussed:

1. Case Study — Ecotourism potential in M.P.
2. Case Study of Bandhavgarh National Park — Ecotourism and Livelihood.
3. Community based ecotourism — Kerwa case study.
4. Concept of Ecotourism.
5. Concept of sustainable livelihood.
6. Course outline and setting the goals.
7. Economic valuation of ecotourism.
8. Ecotourism as a management tool.
9. Ecotourism networking — local, national and international.
10. Ecotourism planning.
11. Environmental auditing in ecotourism.
12. Experience in Ecotourism — global view.
13. Experience sharing — A case study of Seoni.
14. Introspection of tourism and ecotourism policies.
15. Panel discussion — Community participation and livelihood options in ecotourism.
16. Participatory management in Ecotourism.
17. Recreation forests — Innovations in ecotourism.
18. Regional ecotourism planning — Case study of Satpuda — Maikal range.
19. Tools, techniques and methodology in ecotourism.

Field exercises conducted

- Exercise on development of perspective planning for Pachmarhi. Village visit. Case study on livelihood options of ecotourism.
- Field exercise — development of perspective plan for ecotourism in Ratapani sanctuary.
- Field exercise on Kerwa — Livelihood options of ecotourism.
- Field exercise — Van Vihar National Park. Economic Valuation and Environmental Auditing.
- Village visit — Community based ecotourism.

2

OUTCOME OF THE CAPACITY BUILDING EFFORTS

A.K. BHATTACHARYA

2.1 Key Words related to Ecotourism identified by the Participants

The participants were requested to identify all the key words which they could relate to ecotourism and assign these words to one of the five identified categories.

Key Words	*Social*	*Economic*	*Ecological*	*Policy*	*Institutional*
Access				X	
Accommodation	X	X			
Adventure sports				X	
Alternative livelihood	XXX	XXX	X		
Amenities	X				
Animal abundance				X	
Awareness	X				
Awareness of nature	X		X		
Beneficiary	X				
Biodiversity	X	X	XXX		
Biodiversity conservation	X		XX		
Biological awareness	X				X
Biotic pressure	XX				
Boarding		X			
Capacity building	X				
Capital				X	
Carrying capacity	XXX	XXX	XXXXX	XXX	XX
Catering		X		XXX	
Civic sense	X				
Communication	X	X		X	X

Key Words	*Social*	*Economic*	*Ecological*	*Policy*	*Institutional*
Community	X	X			
Community conservation	X				
Community development	X	X			
Community input		X			
Conflict	XX				
Conservation	X		XXX	XX	
Co-operative	X				
Co-ordination					X
Counselling	X				
Culture					X
Culture and tradition	XX				
Data-bank			X		
Development	X				X
Dispersion			X		
Disturbance			X		
Draft plan				X	
Earning	X			X	
Eco-adventure			XX	X	
Eco-development	XX				
Ecofriendly			X		
Ecosystem			X X	X	
Ecotourism			X	XX	
Ecotourism boards					X
Education	X				X
Educational capacity					X
Empowerment	X				
Endangered				X	
Entertainment		X			
Entry point programme				X	
Ethnic values	X				
Fauna			X		
Federations		X			
Fire	X	X	X		
Flora			X		
Food web			X		
Forest	X				
Forest dweller	X				
Government policy	X				
Habitat			X		
Hotspot			X		
Human right	X				
Icon species				X	
Income		X			
Indigenous knowledge	X				

Key Words	*Social*	*Economic*	*Ecological*	*Policy*	*Institutional*
Information				X	
Infrastructure		X		X	X
Institutional origin				X	X
Interface	X				
Learning					X
Livelihood	X	XX			
Lodging		X			
Man power	X	X			
Management		X	X		
Market		X			
Market linkages		X			
Media				X	
Modalities				X	
Monitoring plan				X	
Nature club	X		X		
Nature study				X	
Nature tourism			X		
NGO role					X
Nodal agencies					X
Opportunity		X			
Organisation				X	
Outing	X				
Participation	X	X			
Participatory	XX				X
Planning	X	X	X	X	X
Poaching	X	X		X	X
Pollution			XX		
Population	X				
Potential		X			
Potential sites				X	
Programme sustenance			X		
Promotion of local product		X			
Protected area		X	X		
Protection	X		X	X X	X
Recreation	X	X			
Resolution				X	
Resource development	X	X	X		
Segregation	X				
Self help	X	X			
Skill					X
Social structure	X				
Stakeholder	X				

Key Words	*Social*	*Economic*	*Ecological*	*Policy*	*Institutional*
Surrounding villages		X			
Sustainable development			X		
Tourism		X		X	XX
Tourism policy				X	
Training	X				
Tranquillity			X		
Trekking			X		X
Tribal	X				
Trust building	X				
Unemployment	XX	X		X	
User group	X	X			X
Village committee					X
Village level committee	X				
Visiting		X			
Visitor satisfaction	X	X			
Waste disposal			X		
Wilderness			XX	X	
Zonation			X		

From the analysis of the results, it emerges that the key words getting the maximum ranking are carrying capacity, conversation and alternative livelihood and the social dimension has captured the maximum key words.

Note : X = Number of times the participants has repeated the key word.

2.2. Recommendations for the Ecotourism Development of Kerwa Region—Outside PA Area

Based on the field exercise on Kerwa, a potential ecotourism area, followed by the group discussion the participants have suggested the following issues and the recommendations.

Issues	*Recommendations*
Social issues	
Unemployment	Ecotourism induced. Employment opportunities.
No benefit for the local people from tourism activities	Benefit sharing from the tourism generated income for the local people.
Water scarcity	Upgradation and sinking of wells and bore wells.

Issues	*Recommendations*
Sanitation	Proper awareness of sanitation and hygiene.
Transportation	Bus service should be extended to the village.
Women empowerment	Women should be given a major stake in ecotourism activities which can enhance their economic and social status.
Economic issues	
Income generation	Jobs in ecotourism facilities.
Less economic benefits for the community	Spreading of tourism activities in villages.
No private sector participation in tourism activities	Proper management plan should be prepared and tenders should be floated.
New job opportunities for villagers	Community based ecotourism—activities like boating, rock climbing, angling, trekking, nursery plantations, etc. should be encouraged.
Ecological issues	
Increase in pollution—water and solid waste pollution	Control of pollution by legal and awareness building measures.
Conservation activities	Growing trees, prevention of illegal felling.
Environmental education	Interpretation facilities, study tours, education trails, hoarding.
Fuelwood collection	Shop for the collection and selling of fuelwood, by ecotourism committees.
Nursery	Selling of ornamental and medicinal plants along with fruit bearing trees.

Issues	*Recommendations*
Carrying capacity	Number of visitors should be controlled so that there is less soil erosion, noise pollution, congestion etc.
Follow up activities	Monitoring and evaluation.
Policy issues	
Community based ecotourism	Village ecotourism committees should be constituted and will manage ecotourism activities at the village.
Unrestricted entry of tourists to an area	Imposing of entry fees for the tourists. Restricting the vehicles into tourism area. Developing the parking area and imposing a parking fee.
Fisheries	Provisions for the catching of fishes from the reservoir by the community.
Archaeological Survey of India	Protection of Pathankot cave paintings and Maria Court historical remains to ASI.
Irrigation department	Provision for water in the reservoir throughout the year for tourism purposes.
Trekking trail	Construction of trail should be on the basis of policies of forest department.
Benefit sharing	Proper mechanism for benefit sharing and the utilisation of the saving for development activities.
Controlling of tourist behaviour	Controlling and regulation by legal and awareness building measures, the activities of tourists like alcohol consumption, pollution, cooking and fuelwood consumption etc.

Issues	Recommendations
Institutional issues	
No proper institution for controlling ecotourism activities	Joint Ecotourism Management Committee (JEMC) should be constituted and various sub-committees formed for proper implementation of different activities related to ecotourism.
Other issues	
Capacity building	Capacity building should be carried out for each of the stake-holders.
Local products and artifacts	Marketing and sale of local products and artifacts like flowers, rock carvings, 'rangoli', bamboo products etc.
Religious activities	Fares at Sarotipura cave temple and Dam temple should be properly publicised.

Villagers' Perception of Ecotourism—Kerwa Region

- Villagers know what is tourism as they are educated about it.
- Tourists visit Kerwa dam on Sundays and other holidays. This area is preferred by the college students during the weekdays.
- Two or three people who own a shop in the area are benefited from the tourism activities.
- Villagers are willing to participate in the ecotourism activity.
- There is positive reaction from the tourists.
- Tourism activity will help in income generation.
- Villagers are willing to implement the ecotourism activity at the village level.
- Facilities and capacity building efforts are required for guide training, growing medicinal plants, etc.

- Infrastructure need to be developed, like shops, roads, water facilities, toilets, etc.
- Villagers are willing to work as guides, shopkeepers, labourers, in forest nurseries and facility providers.
- They are ready to work for ecotourism and have a lot of expectation from it for their livelihood.
- There are very few traditional handicrafts in the area, which may be encouraged through ecotourism.
- *Bhajan* groups can be encouraged as a local art group.

2.3. Recommendations about Ratapani Wildlife Sanctuary

The field exercise was conducted in the PA area of Ratapani Sanctuary. The following suggestions were made by the participants.

Issues	*Recommendations*
Social Issues	
Fear of losing the ancestral land	Campaigning by PA managers and revenue department.
Poverty	Poverty removal by Tribal Welfare Department.
Drinking water	Deepening of wells and bore wells by forest department. Damming of streams and raising of 'talabs' (Tanks) and water harvesting structures.
Key persons	Prominent persons to be identified.
Positive impacts due to EDC— • Better fodder production • Fire protection • General forest protection	Further motivation and funding by Forest Department.

Issues	*Recommendations*
Response to ecotourism	Positive response received, motivation in right direction required by Forest Department.
Inclination to implement ecotourism in village	Capacity building, infrastructure development.
Local festivals	Publicity and invitation for tourists, Maintenance of hygiene.
Economic Issues	
Income Generation	Avenues for better marketing of products.
Small landholding which cannot be increased further	Alternative means of livelihood.
Arability of land	Improve irrigation facility.
Seasons of work—July to January	Provide employment from February to June.
Other occupations in lean seasons	In summer collect *Tendu* leaves, *mahua* and make *achar.*
No present benefit from tourism.	Develop minimum rural infrastructure.
Ecological Issues	
Teak Forest	Planting of Frugivorous Trees.
Potable Water for Animals	Gully Plugging, 'Talab', Channel Diversion, 'Bawdi' Clearance.
Ginnaurgarh Fort	Night Stay facility.
Poaching	Patrolling on Foot and Vehicle.
Water Resource	Water Harvesting Structures.
Policy Issues	
Local employment	Sanctuary dwellers be employed for protection, guide, work execution etc.
Restriction of entry into sanctuary.	Develop barriers.

Issues	*Recommendations*
Tourism	New circuit to be created. More areas to be opened, Every vehicle be escorted by guides.
Extension	Widespread and well-connected publicity network.
Follow up activities	Monitoring and evaluation.
Ecotourism as tool for forest management	Legislation and government orders—Speaking guidelines.
Institutional Issues	
Community	All activities should be taken up with the consent and agreed upon by the community.
Community assets	Group formation for generation and maintenance of fund and training
Private agents	Limitation factors for building assets.
Ignorance about ecotourism	Educating about ecotourism.
Other Issues	
Profit sharing	Consensus to be evolved over sharing mechanism.
Local products	Capacity building for the local people.

Villagers perception about ecotourism in Ratapani Wildlife Sanctuary

1. Villagers want that since tourists come to their village and the sanctuary so they should get some economic help.
2. Villagers are not very clear about the concept of ecotourism.
3. Villagers want to engage in ecotourism activities and implement it in their villages.

4. Infrastructure needs to be built for the tourism development.
5. They are willing to let the tourists come and stay in their village but in separate cottages.
6. Villagers want to be a part of ecotourism, as it will boost their livelihood options.
7. Positive reaction from tourists regarding tourism.
8. Expectations from any ecotourism venture—
   - There should be no beggars.
   - Proper training is required.
   - Loan facility should be present.
9. Villagers will be a part of this venture by taking charge of boarding, lodging, housing, site seeing, cooking, etc.
10. There are traditional handicrafts of the area like broom making, mahua beverage, bamboo baskets etc.
11. There are rich flora and fauna existing in the tourism area.
12. There is domestic tourism in the area.
13. Capacity building is required in the case of guides training and shops construction.
14. Traditional jobs are collection of *tendu* leaves, *mahua,* and making *achar.*

Livelihood Benefits from Ecotourism

1. Ecoutorism can be an effective alternative source of income generation.
2. Efforts should be made to improve their understanding and open ways to generate income.
3. With development in an area, they will be improving their living standards.
4. Ecotourism activity will improve the literacy level of the villagers, as basic and primary education will help youngsters to fetch the jobs as guides.
5. Ecotourism will be bringing better infrastructure to an area and will lead to overall development of the area.
6. Villagers will be able to make better use of their natural resources.

2.4 Recommendations for Community Based Ecotourism

Short Term	*Long Term*
Realistic information in EDC about ecotourism	Inviting cross country NGOs for plan and project formulation.
Education and training for the community	Involving ecologists and framing the rules for environmental management.
Facilitation of shelter and hygienic accommodation for the tourists	Evaluation of long term result and change of direction of planning.
Making required all basic amenities for the tourists	Inviting other stakeholders like entrepreneurs, public-private partnership.
Sufficient funding for the implementation of the plans	Improving existing resources and adding more visitors attraction.
Supervision of plans, advice and formulation by experts	Legislative restriction on tourism zone.
Motivation for ecotourism in right direction.	Regional and national level promotion.
Funding for small scale infrastructure.	
Provide subsidies, grants, bank loans.	
Capitalising available resource and marketing.	
Checks on vandalism.	
Local level publicity about facility.	

2.5 Ecotourism Module for Rorighat, Panchmarhi

Through the field exercise in the PA of Panchmarhi, community based ecotourism module was suggested by the participants for the Rorighat village of Pachmarhi.

Introduction

Rorighat is a small village of Pagara Panchayat. The village falls *en route* to the God Shiva Temple in Kajri and located within the geographical location of the Satpuda National Park. The participants of the workshops were asked to analyse the ecotourism potentials, problems and possible solutions for this area during a field exercise. As it is situated in the proximity of Pachmarhi, there is great possibility for developing this area as a diversion zone for tourists. It is also a place near Bhopal, thereby increasing its potential as a tourist site. The following are the findings of the same:

Current Scenario

1. Village inhabitants—100% Korku : Homogeneous
2. Main occupation
   - Agriculture—maize, wheat, Jowar (for self-consumption)
   - Animal husbandry—ghee making
   - Business—broom, basket, *patal* making, honey extraction, pilgrimage tourism, mahua distillery.
   - Labourers in the forest.
3. Already exposed to tourism activities
4. Level of education is low : up to fifth standard and women are uneducated
5. Strong EDC exists
6. Skills exist : "basket", *patal, chatai,* broom making, folk song —"Shetam", folk dance – "Dandinach"
7. Conservation activities : through EDC ; check dams, jungle roads, water holes
8. Women involve just for name sake in developmental activities
9. Type of tourists :
   - Pilgrimage tourism – Nagpanchmi (8 days), Baisakhi (3 days), Rangpanchmi (1 day).
   - Tourist to Bori—12-15 vehicles per week in a season.
10. Benefits derived: 5-10 Rupees per person per day.

11. Present level of income—annual income 8 lakh at the rate of Rs.16,000 by the sale of NTFP—Daily wage earning.
12. Socio-economic status of the village
    - Households – 45
    - Population – 300 (adults 124)
    - Cattle population – 126
    - Landholders – 19 acres
    - Landholdings – 1 acre

Basic Infrastructure required

- Roads
- Electricity
- Shops/Hotels/Cottages
- Picnic area
- Basic sanitation and drinking water

Tourism related Local People Employment Ventures

- Tour guides
- Restaurant handling
- Shop owners
- Cottage industry
- General employment

Expected revenue generation per person per day inclusive of boarding lodging and sight-seeing should be Rs. 150.

Objectives of Study

- Strategy for increased income generation of the village through Community Based Ecotourism.

Existing Community—Ecotourism Interface

(1) Social capital—Homogeneous, no conflicts, socially acceptable, rich in cultural heritage.

(2) Financial capital—extracting economic benefits during the festivals from the tourists.

(3) Physical capital—approach road, temples, Bori National Park.

(4) Natural capital—mountains, valleys, perennial water, forest, NTFP, wild life.

(5) Human capital—manpower.

Scope and Potential

Scenic beauty, forests wildlife, water harvesting, required willingness and manpower to involve in ecotourism activities.

Strengths

Homogeneous, road connection, nearer to Panchmarhi, perennial water source, EDC, law abiding, less expectation from the way of religious congregation, Bori N.P.

Weaknesses

Relatively less aware, poverty, illiteracy, poor medical and health facilities, lack of transport, no electricity, no settled agriculture, poor yields, obsolete technology, soil erosion, lack of marketing of ecotourism potential area.

Pilgrimage—Tourism Linkages

- Make village into a transit hub of pilgrims and tourists.
- Provide ecofriendly infrastructure for boarding and lodging.
- Grow fruit, medicinal plants and vegetables for sale.
- Organise cultural shows/folk dances.

Need for Capacity Building

- Training on harvesting and value addition of NTFP.
- Education on ecotourism aspects.
- Marketing and sale.
- Strengthening of EDC.
- Soil conservation and water harvesting.
- Adult literacy.

- Improved agricultural practices, horticultural cultivation of medicinal plants.

Role of Village Level Institutions

- EDC—Sensitising on conservation of forest and wildlife.
- SHG—To generate income.
- School education.
- PHC—Health.
- NGO—motivation.

Linkage with Other Stakeholders

- With Forest Department for manpower and conservation.
- With pilgrims and tourists for food, shelter and guidance.
- With NGO for motivation.

Revenue Generation

Entry fees as decided by the EDC.

Community Organisation and Participation

Community sharing of benefits and responsibilities. Village ecodevelopment committee exists. Sharing of benefits and responsibilities can be in the following ways:

(1) Biodiversity conservation—cleaning of land, slash-burning for agriculture.
(2) Erection of community sheds by the committees for five days depending on the number of pilgrims stay.
(3) Co-operative support facility extension.
(4) Co-operative marketing.
(5) Sharing of benefits.
(6) Contribution to the 'common welfare fund' by the members.
(7) Capacity building by the committee (training as guides drivers, handicrafts etc.).

Staff

Feedback and monitoring

2.6 Ecotourism Perspective Plan for Pachmarhi Plateau

The participants proposed the perspective plan for the tourism development at Pachmarhi as an output of the field visit.

Background

Only hill station in M.P. centrally located, near to Maharashtra and Gujarat State. It is of historical and mythological importance, erstwhile summer capital of M.P., spacious, unpolluted, untapped potential enough scope for expansion located in wildlife sanctuary suitable for visit throughout the year. It also has religious significance.

The field exercise for the participants of the workshop was to analyse the ecotourism potential and problems and on its basis prepare a perspective ecotourism management plan for the area.

Existing Potential

- Infrastructure—Approachable by road and accommodation available.
- Scenic recreational, religious, historical, wildlife spots available and rich in flora and fauna.

Objectives of Perspective Plan

- Recreation and entertainment.
- Environmental education and awareness building.
- Employment generation.
- Economic benefits.
- People's participation.
- Conservation of flora and fauna.
- Promoting adventure tourism and nature trails.
- Sustainability by generating revenue and ploughing back by creating revolving fund.

Suggested Plan

(a) Infrastructure development

- Publicity/tourist information centre
- Improving approach road

- Accommodation—eco-lodges, resorts, hotels, cottages, dormitories
- Transportation
- Hospitals
- Shopping complex
- Development of lakes for boating
- Gardens/parks
- Renovation of temples
- Watch towers
- Regular water and electricity supply
- Waste management
- Conducted tours with local people as guides

(b) Expansion of tourist activities

- Rock climbing
- Trekking
- Site seeing of wild animals in tourism zones
- More hoarding and tourist information infrastructure
- Undertaking plays for awareness building
- Distribution of seedlings as "*prasad*" in temples.
- Adoption of trees

(c) Community participation and addressing livelihood issues

- Local people as ecotourism guides
- Employment generation
- Cultural shows, folk shows
- Growing and sale of medicinal and ornamental plants and also fruits
- Cultivation and sale of NTFP products
- Sale of handicrafts

(d) Implementation

- Forest Department as nodal agency
- Deputy conservator of forest cadre officer to be posted
- Co-ordination with local civic body, PWD, health, tourism hotel, federations, tour operators, ASI, police, endowments, other departments, etc.
- Vested with regulatory and financial powers

(e) Sources of revenue

- Toll gates
- Entry / gate fees
- Sale of seedling stickers, badges, caps, key chains, etc.
- Film shooting / photography
- Local tax collection
- Temple earnings (trust)
- Establish Pachmarhi Ecotourism development fund and recycle the revenue earned.

(f) Cost benefit analysis

S.No.	*Year*	*Number of tourists*	*Revenue (Rs.)*	*Expenditure (Rs.)*
1	2002-03	1.25 lakhs	0.22 crores	0.50 crores
2	2011-12	5 lakhs	2.50 crores	1.50 crores

There are a number of indirect benefits, most of which cannot be quantified.

(g) SWOT Analysis

Strengths

- Only hill station located near the centre of the state
- Scenic beauty
- Historical and mythological importance
- Spacious, unpolluted
- Enough scope for expansion
- Located near wildlife sanctuary
- Suitable for visit throughout the year
- Religious significance
- Rich flora and fauna
- Approachable by roads
- Good accommodation available

Weaknesses

- Pollution
- Threat to ecosystem

Opportunities

- Employment generation
- Awareness building and sensitising the tourists

- Involving the local communities
- Area development
- Optimum utilisation of resources
- Revenue generation

Threats

- Over-utilisation of resources
- Increase in pollution
- Depleting water resources
- Misuse of the area
- Number of tourists above the carrying capacity of the area
- Threat to the flora and fauna
- Lack of benefits to the local community

Expectations

1. *Tourists*
    - Entertainment
    - Security
    - Economy
    - Services
2. *Local inhabitants*
    - Socio-economic development
    - Roads and school
    - Drinking water
    - Communication facilities
    - Means of livelihood
    - Maintaining cultural heritage on sustainable basis
3. *Environmentalists*
    - Conservation of biodiversity
    - Check forest fires
    - Check soil erosion
    - Effective water harvesting

How to go about it

- Plan
- Publicize

- Create
- Market
- Institutionalize
- Maintain

Strategy to Develop Ecotourism

1. Infrastructure—roads, electricity, sanitation, water.
2. Capacity building and training—agroforestry, cottage industry, management of ecotourism facilities.
3. Facilitator—IIFM/NGO, funding at initial stage, capacity building training, institutionalization for project, initiation, implementation, monitoring and evaluation/Forest Department.
4. Value addition—introduction of adventure sports
   - Eco-resort within village
   - Package tour—Pachmarhi, Rorighat and Bori
   - Cultural (Pseudo mela)—Chauki dhani
   - Handicrafts.
5. Benefit sharing—venture initiated by EDC—plough back the profit—conservation activity—local economy recharge—maintenance of facilities.
6. Marketing—networking with tour operators, hoteliers, Tourism Department, institution, corporate tie-up.
7. Facilities to be provided based on the buying capacity of tourists
   - Grade I - Upper class
   - Grade II - Middle class
   - Grade III - Student/Rural people
8. Strategic management in waste water and land.
9. Emergency preparedness—Medical, fire, security (Law and order).

2.7 Ecotourism Auditing—Van Vihar National Park, Bhopal

(Documentation by Vandana Saksena, A.K. Bhattacharya)

Questionnaire Survey

The methodology included survey through :

- Questionnaires directly supplied to the visitors.

- Direct observations of the visitors' activities (spot survey).
- Questionnaire survey in individual and in focus groups.

In all 175 questionnaires were supplied to the visitors entering to the park from both the gates. They were requested to co-operate in giving proper and patient replies to the questions asked in the annexure.

The demographic information about the visitors such as the age, sex, education, profession, occupation, place of origin and their income profile have been presented in both tabular and graphical form.

(a) ***Age Group and Sex Ratio*:** Seventy-five per cent of the visitors to the park are in the age group of 18-30, followed by 62 per cent in the age group of 35-50. In the age group of 50 and above only 32 per cent visitors come to the park. The minimum arrival is of the visitors below 18 years who are mostly children and just teenagers. Seventy-two per cent of males and 30 per cent females visit the national park.

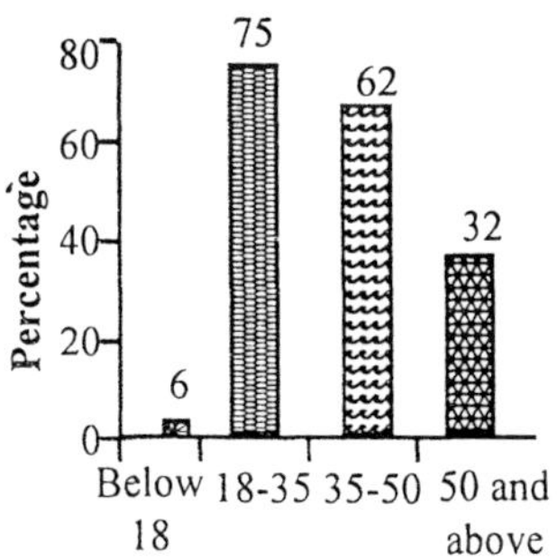

Age Group

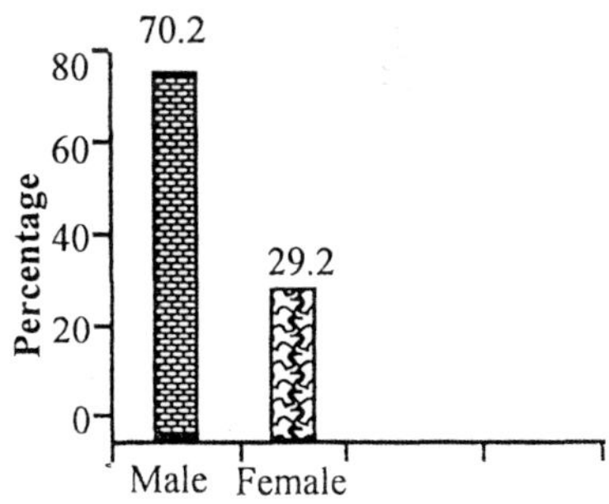

Sex Ratio

(b) ***Occupation*:** The visitors' survey result indicates that 20 per cent visitors are government employees belonging to teaching, LIC, Banking sectors. Twenty-four per cent visitors are from the private sector companies, while 16 per cent are businessmen who are involved in export and in travel business. Remaining 40 per cent are students, housewives and retired persons who are frequent visitors.

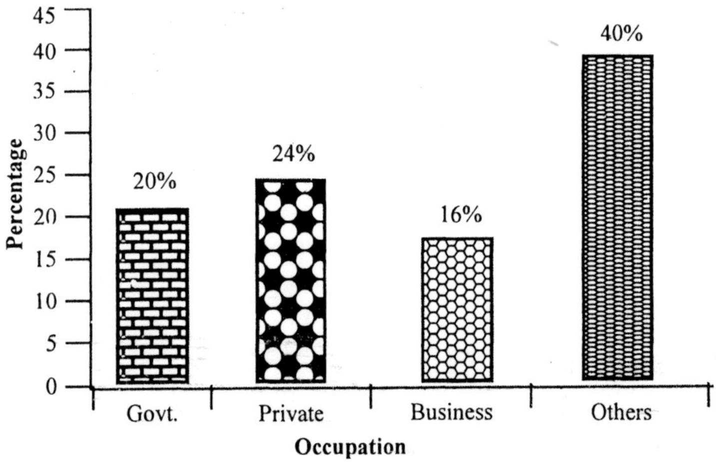

(c) *Qualifications*: Among the total visitors coming to the Park, 11 per cent visitors are educated below 12th standard, most of them are students. Forty-three per cent are graduates and postgraduates. Thirty-five per cent visitors were found to be technically and professionally qualified comprising of engineers, diploma holders, doctors, lawyers, chartered accountants etc.

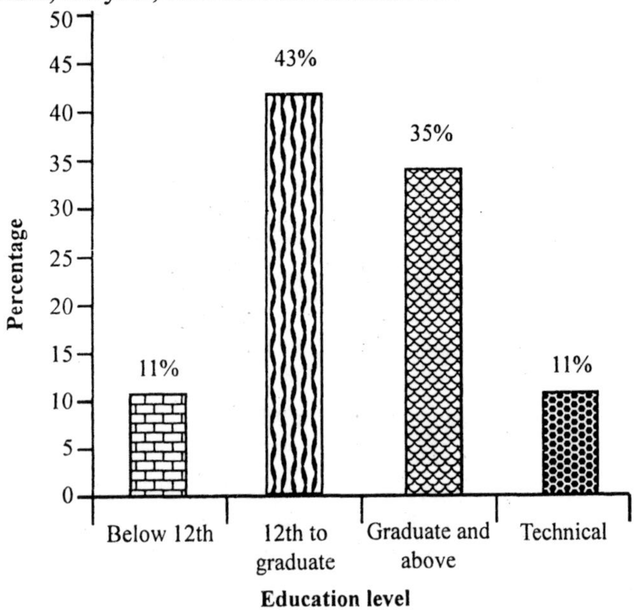

(d) ***Income***: While 71 per cent visitors responded to the queries of income, 29 per cent were reluctant to respond. Of the 71 per cent, 56 per cent visitors come from income group of more than Rs.1 lakh annually, while 11 per cent come from the income between Rs. 50,000 to 1,00,000 per year. A very small section of visitors belong to the income group of less than Rs. 50,000, their percentage being only four.

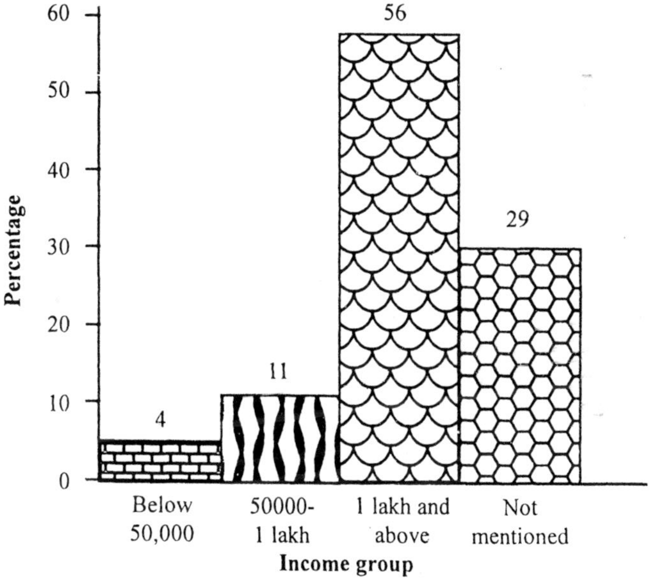

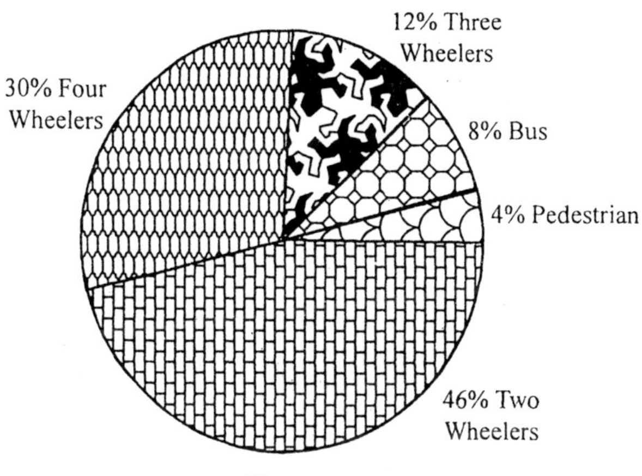

Transport

(e) ***Mode of Transport:*** The survey indicates that 46 per cent people visit Van Vihar with their two-wheelers comprising of scooters, motorbikes and mopeds. Thirty per cent visit with their own four-wheelers, while about 12 per cent visitors come in three-wheelers (auto-rickshaws). Of the remaining 12 per cent, 8 per cent enjoy the visit inside the park in Van Vihar owned battery operated bus and only 4 per cent see the park walking without using any vehicle. The battery-operated bus provides an environmental friendly atmosphere to the visitors.

2.8. Visitors' Perception

The visitors' perception was captured on the basis of their interest towards ecotourism.

(a) *Purpose of Visit*

Response to the purpose of visit was based on ranking system. The result indicates that 88 per cent people come to Van Vihar for watching wild life. Eighty per cent of the people gave priority to love for nature. Remaining people go to VanVihar for scenic beauty followed by outing and close by picnic spot. The local residents of Bhopal specifically bring their guests, relatives and friends to the Park for showing them the wild animals, birds, reptiles and the scenic beauty of hills and the lake. This occupies the last rank of the purpose of visit under tourist perception.

WILDLIFE (88%)

↓

LOVE FOR NATURE (80%)

↓

SCENIC BEAUTY (72%)

↓

CLOSE BY PICNIC SPOT (40%)

↓

OUTING (26%)

↓

OTHERS (16%)

(b) *Number of visits per year*

"How often do you come here?" was the question which was responded by the people in the following manner as given on next page.

The sample data indicates that 42 per cent of the people visit Van Vihar once in a year, followed by 22 per cent twice a year, 6 per cent thrice a year, and 4 per cent four, five, six times per year. Ten per cent local people visit this place more than 10 times a year. 2 per cent visitors did not respond properly.

(c) *What fascinated the most*

When the question of liking was raised to the visitors they gave priority to wildlife (32%), followed by natural beauty (25%), lake view (20%), surrounding of the area (12%) etc. Very few visitors liked interpretation centre (4%) from where they could have obtained most of the information about Van Vihar and wild life. Rest of the visitors (7%) did not respond. The percentage is shown in the table below. The hill view and the natural sight of the Upper Lake also fascinated the visitors very much.

Sl. No.	*Number of visits per year*	*%*
1.	1	42
2.	2	22
3.	3	6
4.	4	4
5.	5	4
6.	6	4
7.	10	6
8.	More than 10	10
9.	Did not respond	2

Sl. No.	*Responses*	*%*
1	Wildlife	32
2	Natural beauty	25
3	Lake-view	20
4	Surroundings	12
5	Interpretation centre	04
6	Did not respond	07

(d) *Awareness about ecotourism*

Only 48 per cent visitors responded in positive about awareness towards ecotourism. According to them "ecotourism is travelling to nature, tour to ecology, visiting natural places having beauty

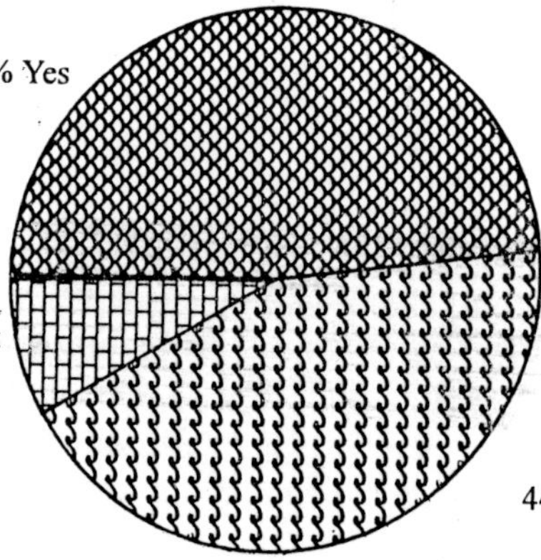

helps in developing human concern to protect nature and ecosystem, love towards nature and nearness to its surroundings which includes the attraction of wildlife". For some it is a good source of earning revenue from foreign exchange. Significantly 44 per cent of the visitors has no idea of ecotourism, while remaining 8 per cent did not show any interest in responding to this question.

(e) *Awareness about the codes of conduct of Ecotourism*

From the survey it is clear that very few people have knowledge of codes of conduct of ecotourism. According to them codes of conduct comprise of the rules and regulations of Wildlife Protection Act, Environment Protection Act pertaining to air, water, noise and solid waste, non-disposal of plastics and polythene bags, littering, noise free environment, and promotion of plantation. Majority of the people do not have any idea about such codes. As graphical representation clearly indicates that only 10 per cent visitors are aware about the codes of conduct of ecotourism. Sixty per cent people do not know anything about the codes, while a substantial 30 per cent did not respond to the question.

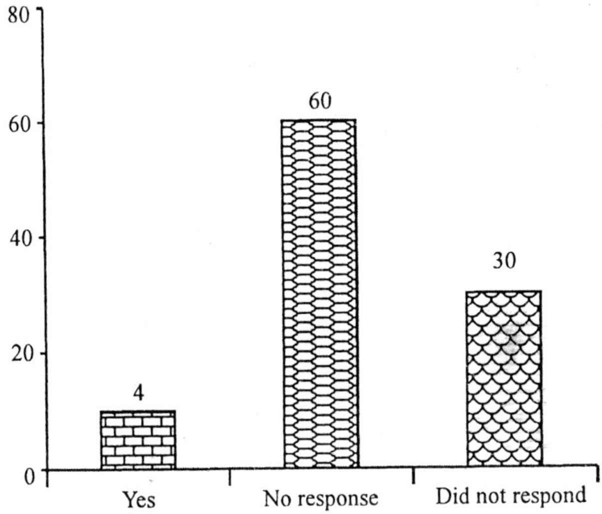

(f) *Guidelines and instruction by the park staff*

Forty eight percent visitors confirmed of having received the guidelines/instructions regarding tourism in the park, while 26per cent people strongly denied. Remaining 26 per cent did not respond.

Sl. No.	*Responses*	*%*
1	Yes	48
2	No	26
3	Did not respond	26

(g) *Food brought by visitors in the park*

In reply to the question "what do you bring to eat during your visit?" Forty-eight per cent people replied they bring fast food.

Nine per cent people bring cooked food while the percentage of containers used to bring eating material is 43.

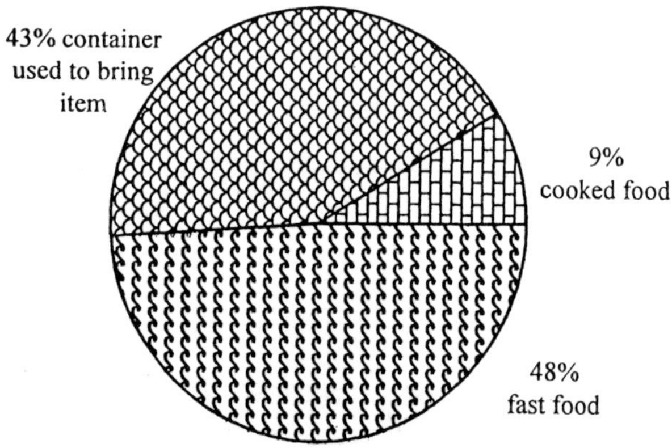

(h) ***Use of wrappers /carry bags/polythenes***

The visitors who bring cooked and fast food said that they put the left over food and used paper, polythene etc. into the dustbins. Their percentage is 46, while 6 per cent throw these waste material by the side of the lake, 12 per cent carry them back. The remaining 34 per cent throw them here and there or anywhere.

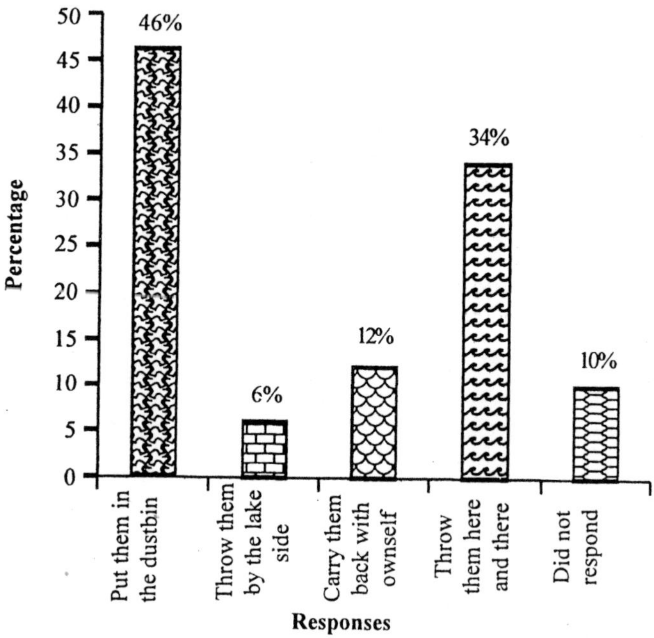

(i) *Garbage bins*

Eighty-two per cent visitors find garbage bins in the park area affixed at proper places, while 18 per cent did not notice bins in the park.

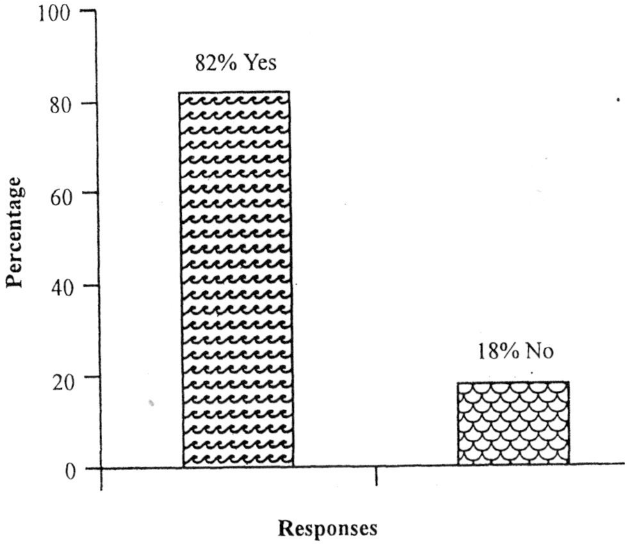

(j) *Facilities in Van Vihar*

Sixty-six per cent visitors feel that the facilities inside the Van Vihar are inadequate, 26 per cent are satisfied with the adequacy of facilities and rest 8 per cent did not respond.

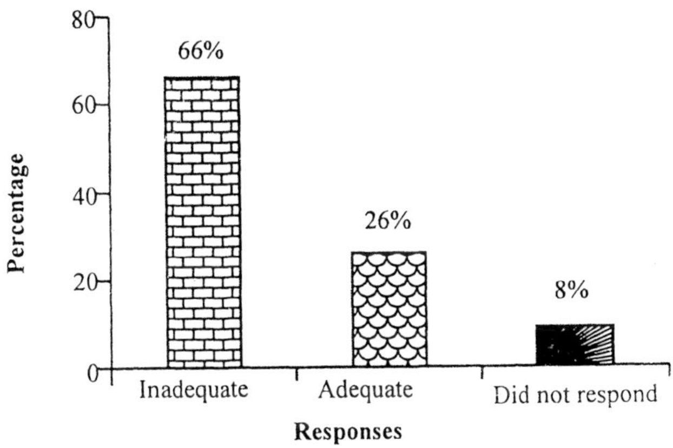

(k) *Guide*

Ninety per cent visitors say that they do not find/get any guide who could guide or instruct them properly about the park, ecotourism and wild animals. Only 5 per cent visitors told that some park staff did guide them a little bit about the wild animals and natural surroundings. Five per cent did not respond.

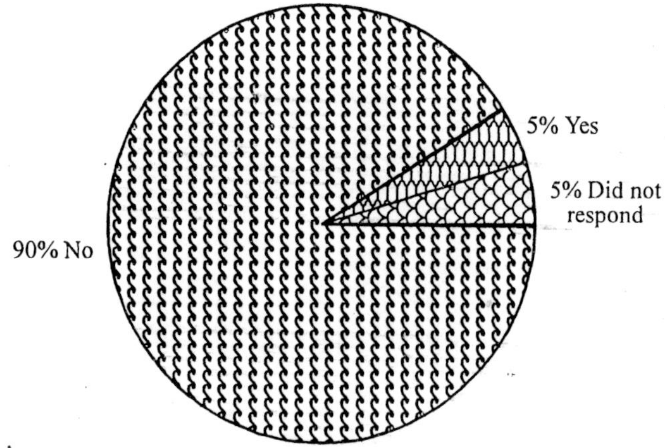

(l) *Willingness to pay for the guides*

As evident earlier that there was great need of guides in the park,

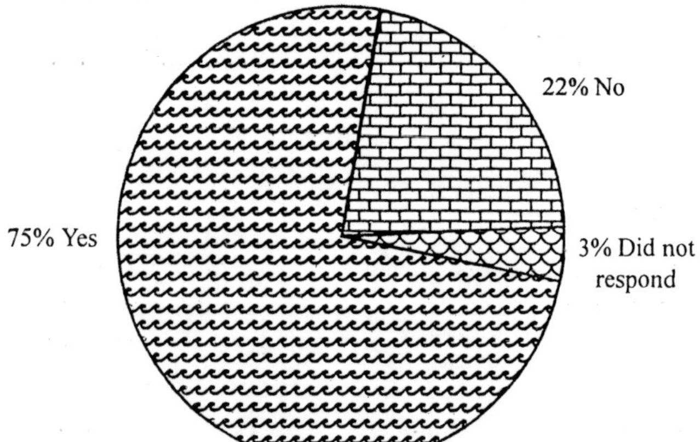

75 per cent visitors are willing to pay fee for the guides during their visit. Only 22 per cent visitors showed reluctance for payment to guides. Three per cent did not respond.

(m) ***Awareness Generation***

According to 78 per cent visitors Van Vihar is a proper site of awareness generation as well as getting education about wildlife conservation. Of the remaining people about 18 per cent do not think so. They come only for recreation purpose or just for outing. Rest of the people did not respond.

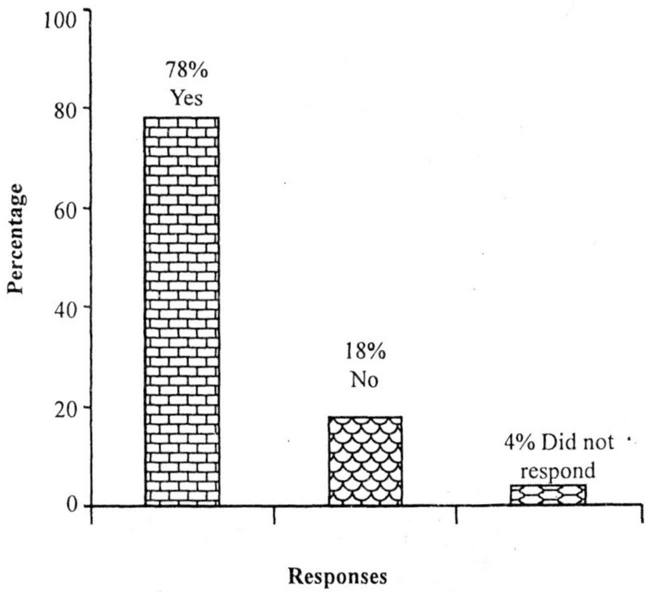

(n) ***Interpretation Centre***

18 per cent visitors get adequate information from the interpretation centre, known as Vihar Vithika, 54 per cent get partially adequate information, while 24 per cent are totally unsatisfied from it. They complained that there was none to either welcome or guide them or provide useful and interesting information about the park.

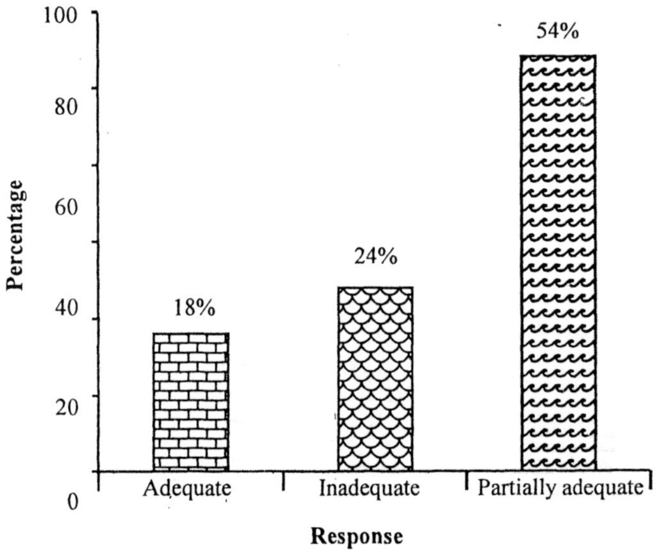

(o) *Public Involvement in Park Management*

80 per cent visitors showed their interest in park management if they are given chance to do so. Some people did not show any willingness to involve themselves in park management. Only 10 per cent did not respond properly.

(p) *Contribution of Public in Park Management*

The people showed lot of interest in park management activities. They gave first rank to a joint committee of forest staff and people (75 per cent), followed by 68 per cent visitors suggesting/educating others to maintain healthy environment in the park. Thirty-eight per cent of people were interested in participation in management activities while 33 per cent were keen for maintaining cleanliness and health of park. (see figure on next page)

(q) *Merits and Demerits of the Park*

Observations enumerated in table on the next page reveals that visitors like the Park for its good roads, calm and quite atmosphere, natural beauty, nearness to lakeside, and good wildlife. The visitors felt the entry fee to be on the higher side. Safe drinking water

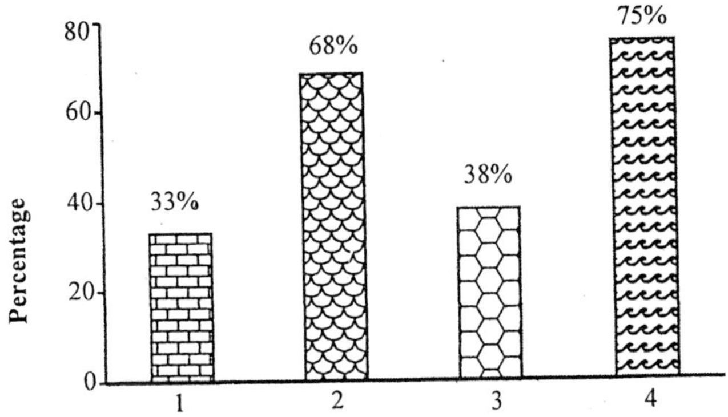

1. By maintaining cleanliness
2. By suggesting/educating others
3. Participation in management
4. Committee of staff and people

problem was observed during their visit; they also marked absence of a canteen for refreshment. Visitors were not happy on the proper management of wildlife particularly about ill feeding the animals. None of the visitors expressed satisfaction on the maintenance of toilets and public convenience. Whatever toilets are available they are very shabby and dirty. There is also no water facility available inside the toilets. As regards the noise and air pollution visitors expressed annoyance over allowing diesel vehicles inside the park. One of the demerits of the park expressed by visitors is the absence of sit outs and covered sitting huts for resting while covering a long distance of nearly 5 km on foot.

Merits	*Demerits*
Good natural beauty	Ticket cost is high
Good wildlife	Shortage of drinking water
Near to Lakeview	Absence of guide
Close by picnic spot	Absence of canteen
Water beauty is an additional attraction of the park	Poor maintenance of wildlife
Calm and quite atmosphere	Noise and air pollution due to entry of vehicle inside the park
Roads are well maintained and neat and clean	Very shabby and dirty toilets
	No proper place for resting and sitting

(r) *Deterioration of environment*

Most of the people visiting the park were generally confused about deterioration of Park's environment. They have not carefully noticed marked difference in the environment of the past *vis-a-vis* the present. However, some of the local and regular visitors did feel that the air pollution in the park had increased *vis-a-vis* the past. According to them the reason of this change is the entry of vehicular traffic inside the park. Besides, the number of visitors has also increased considerably.

(s) *Difficulties and Facilities*

The visitors encountered many difficulties while seeing the wildlife inside the Park. It was the general complaint of the visitors that they were not able to get safe drinking water. Guides were also not available for proper information about the fauna and flora of the Park. They said that there was no proper person to provide them information about Van Vihar. Children accompanied with the visitors could not get anything to eat when they felt hungry during the visit as it took quite a lot of time to see the wild animals coming out in the open.

The visitors suggested following facilities :

Facilities in ranking order

1. Trained guide.
2. Proper drinking water facility at short distances.
3. There is need of eco-friendly canteen in the park.
4. Camera should be allowed inside the park free of cost.
5. Battery operated bus fare should be reduced.
6. A cyber café and telephone booths should be introduced.
7. Pictures of wildlife should be put on sale.

(t) *Suggestions*

Suggestions and opinions of the visitors towards conservation values and improvements in the park as follows :

Suggestions by the visitors for better management of the Park

1. A money collection box should be kept in the Park for

collection of the wildlife fund so as to enable the visitors to donate or contribute generously towards it.

2. Nature camps for awareness generation should be organized on regular basis.
3. In order to earn foreign exchange proper publicity be made to attract foreign tourists towards ecotourism attraction in the park.
4. The permission fee to carry cameras should not be charged.
5. Signboards and hoardings should be put up at prominent places inside the park carrying useful instructions and messages displayed properly in Hindi and English for the visitors.
6. An officer of a senior rank from the Forest Department should keep regular vigil over the activities and quality of food supplied to the wild animals.
7. Fare of the battery operated bus should be reduced by 50 per cent.
8. The present visiting time to the Park should be increased by an hour in the afternoon.
9. Educated trained guides be appointed in the Park.
10. Forest staff should take daily action for progress and maintenance of Park and upkeeping of wildlife.
11. A flower garden be raised and developed by the side of the lake.
12. Diesel vehicles should be strictly prohibited to enter the Park.
13. The number of dustbins should be increased and distance between two bins be conveniently kept.
14. The toilets of the Park should be cleaned daily.
15. There should be resting huts for visiting public.
16. The Park should remain open for visitors throughout the day.
17. There is need of a canteen in the Park.
18. There should be audio-video film shows on wildlife nature attractions including the lakeside beauty.

Forest Staff

Difference between tourism and ecotourism

Most of the forest staff distinguish tourism with ecotourism only by vegetation, wild animals and the nature. Some of the prominent staff members believe that the modern lifestyle is driving people towards this type of tourist entertainment, pure air, water, serenity and tranquillity which according to them are main advantages of ecotourism because artificially one cannot create natural resource and atmosphere. Parking space for vehicles, cleaning of roads from the stockyard, provision of guides, safety of wild animals and their natural habitat make the difference between tourism and eco-tourism.

The lower staff of the Department appears to be highly confused about ecotourism. The responses received from them show that they are totally ignorant about its real concept. Analyzing the data it is found that only a small section of the lower staff knows about the difference between tourism and ecotourism. Some of them do not have an independent opinion of their own.

Ecotourism codes of conduct

Seventy-five per cent of the staff have no idea about the codes of conduct of ecotourism and it is only the 25 per cent staffers who have some idea about the codes. Even they confine there understanding only upto "dos and dont's" about the wild animals and vegetation. However they are aware about the Wildlife Conservation Act.

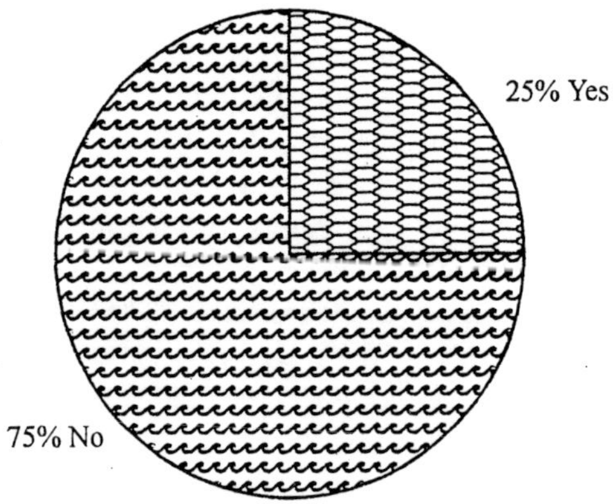

Departmental circulars and guidelines

The response to the question pertaining to departmental circulars and guidelines and park management suggest that 62 per cent have no idea about any circulars and guidelines concerning this subject. Only 38 per cent have some idea about them. It is gathered that only senior officials have the idea about the circulars and guidelines. When asked about the workshops and seminars on ecotourism most of the staff members replied in negative. A very small section of senior staff members attended some or the other sort of training and seminars related to ecotourism.

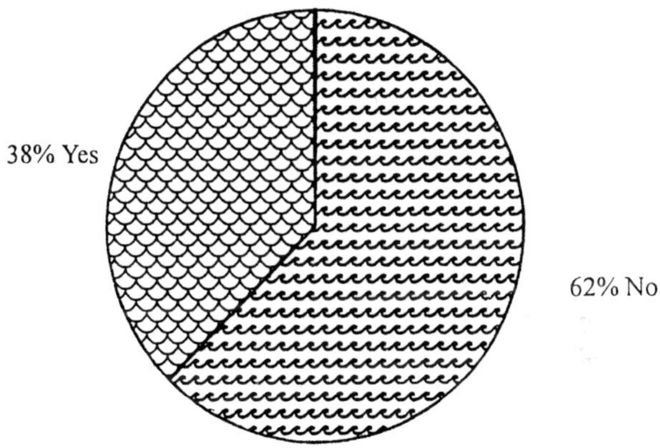

Expectations from the visitors

About 62 per cent staff people expect the visitors to follow rules and regulations as well as instructions about Van Vihar besides keeping the Park clean and green without spreading dirt here and there. Responsible staff (37.5%) want visitors to co-operate with them with decency and decorum without entering into avoidable discussions. About 12 per cent expect that people visiting the Park should not make loud noise and avoid littering while moving. They also expect that the visitors should not approach nearer to the animals or tease them. Instead, they should help conserving the wildlife besides promoting tourism.

Sl. No.	Expectations	%
1	Do not tease the animal	12.5
2	Do not throw polythene bags inside the park	12.5
3	Follow rules and regulations of Van Vihar	62.5
4	Keep park clean and green Do not spread dirt	62.5
5	Avoid misbehaviour with park staff	37.5
6	Cooperation and decency during the visit	12.5
7	Sympathetic approach towards animals	25
8	Promote tourism	25
9	Help conserve the wildlife	25
10	Maintain peace, avoid shouts	12.5
11	No littering	12.5

Problems created by the visitors

Sl. No.	Problems	%
1	Blowing horns	62.5
2	Rash driving	75
3	Rough behaviour	12.5
4	Demanding ticket out of queue	12.5
5	Teasing animals	75
6	Try to go near the animals	12.5
7	Garbaging/littering	25
8	Noise pollution	25

Expectations of the visitors

Almost all the forest staff have some ideas about the expectations of the visitors as shown in the following table:

Sl. No.	*Expectations*	%
1	To see animals specially white tiger	62.5
2	Lower entry fee	25
3	Minimum rules and regulations	25
4	Resting places	25
5	Food facility	25
6	Public convenience	25
7	Safe drinking water	25
8	Maximum information about Park from the staff	62.5
9	Seeing animals in morning	37.5
10	Good behaviour from the staff	50

Potential threats to the environment of Van Vihar

According to the Park staff the potential threats of environment are polythene bags, police firing range near the Park, horn blowing and noise pollution, diesel vehicles, smoking inside the Park, *gutkha pouch,* intoxication, growing of Parthenium and lantana, animal abuse by the visitors, littering and rash driving.

Sl. No.	*Potential threats*	%
1	Diesel vehicles	25
2	Polythene bags	75
3	Smoking	25
4	*Gutka pouch*	12.5
5	Intoxication	12.5
6	Police firing range near the park	50
7	Horn blowing and noise pollution	37.5
8	Growing of Parthenium and lantana	25
9	Animal abuse	12.5
10	Feeding by tourists to animals	12.5
11	Littering	12.5
12	Rash driving	12.5

Suggestions to promote ecotourism in Van Vihar

The forest staff suggest that ecotourism can be promoted in Van Vihar National Park by plantation, resting place, safe drinking water, slide show, website of Van Vihar national park, special tourist buses, co-ordination with the State Tourism Corporation for the promotion of ecotourism, creation of ecotypes, trained guides, advertisement through TV and newspapers.

2.8 Community Based Ecotourism

Module for community based ecotourism for operationalisation

- Form village ecotourism committee for management
- Training camps for upgrading their skills
- Government agencies/NGOs to help them in securing loans for the purpose of creating infrastructure
- Government agencies to provide the enforcement authority to the committees
- Every eco-worker to deposit 10 per cent of his earnings in village development fund for sustainability

Tourists

Willing to pay for	Beneficiary (community or not)
Transport	Maybe
Eatables	Yes
Comforts	Yes
Accommodation facilities	Yes
Amusement	Yes
Information/guides	Yes

Community benefits

Objectives

I. More income
II. Increased well-being
III. Reduced vulnerability
IV. Improved food security
V. More sustainable use of natural resources

Benefits

1. *Direct benefits—incentive with cash*

- Fees
- Fines
- Compensation
- Grants
- Loans
- Revolving funds
- Wages
- Employment

2. *Direct incentives in kind*

- Food
- Animals
- Access to resource areas where sustainable harvesting is a management objective

3. *Indirect fiscal incentive*

- Tax incentives
- Security
- Insurance

4. *Indirect service incentives as community benefits*

- Means of earning a living—as an alternative means of livelihood
- Outside service—to improve their productivity marketing facility—tie up with sale
- Community development—education, health, family planning, sanitation, community centre, electricity, roads, market, water supply.
- Agricultural inputs
  - Rehabilitate soil
  - Introduction of best yield hybrid seeds, medicinal plants, etc.
- Improved uses of resources—like improved stove design, bio gas plant, smokeless 'chulhas.'
- Cultivation and harvesting of native biological diversity for profit
- Education and training.

Maximising the Benefits from Ecotourism

Maximising the Community benefits

Strategy	*Action*
Infrastructure	Government / Private enterprises
Basic Facilities	Village community
Employment	Private and Community
Benefit Sharing	Government / Private/ Community
Identifying Non-Potential Sites	Private / Community
Value Addition to Local Articles/ Culture	Community with technical assistance
Publicity	- Brochures, leaflets and seminars by forest department - Different media to be used - Experts to be roped in
Bringing Different Stakeholders Together	Conflict Management
Development of Local Handicrafts etc.	- Improving local skills - Development or market for local product
Linking of Places with Tourist Importance with Ecotourism in the Area	- Identification of sites - Development of these sites - Eco-friendly infrastructure
Community Participation and Capacity Building	Training
Community Benefits	- Identify the communities - Empowerment of communities through training and capacity building on ecotourism
Effective Institutional Mechanism	- Participatory planning - Participatory implementation
Improvement of Natural Vegetation	- Remove weeds - Tending natural viable root stock - Gap planting with native system

Strategy	*Action*
Watershed Management	- Effective soil moisture conservation - Deepening of ponds
Infrastructure	- Strengthening of existing interpretation centres - Signboards on wildlife and nature - Handicraft sale counter
Other Community Benefits	- Guide services - Handicrafts - Transport - Joy rides (Pony rides, bullock cart rides) - Catering – local delicacies - Boarding

2.10 Exercise on the Proposed Course Outline for Ecotourism

The exercise was conducted to design a course on Ecotourism. The draft course outline was prepared by Ralf Buckley of Australia.

What should the course cover

1. *Introduction*

- Relations between tourism and the natural environment
- Links and dependencies: products, marketing, impacts, economics
- The tourism industry: critical issues from an environmental perspective
- The natural environment: critical issues from a business perspective
- The social and cultural environment: critical issues from business and conservation perspectives

2. *Components of Ecotourism*

- Natural setting and/or nature-based products
- Sustainable or minimal-impact technology and management
- Environmental education and interpretation
- Direct or indirect contribution to conservation

3. *Ecotourism as an Industry Sector*

- NEAT and ACE: integration of nature, adventure and cultural and ecotourism
- Trends and patterns in tourist demands and in tourism products, packaging and marketing

4. *Ecotourism Entrepreneurs*

- Relevant skills and background
- Identifying an opportunity
- Is it ecotourism?
- Access
- Expertise
- Infrastructure
- Licensing
- Marketing
- Seasonality
- Capital, fixed and variable operator costs

5. *Ecotourism Operations Management*

- Equipment and technology
- Environmental management
- Staff skills and training
- Environmental audit and ecotourism accreditation

6. *Ecotourism Guiding*

- Technical skills, people skills and career structure
- The critical role of the guide
- Effective interpretation

7. *Ecotourism and Land Management*

- Managing tourism and ecotourism in parks and protected areas
- Ecotourism on other public lands
- Ecotourism on private lands
- Ecotourism as a source of park funding
- Licensing and accreditation for operators and guides
- Monitoring and managing environmental impacts

8. *Ecotourism and Communities*

- Community coherence, conflicts and representation
- Community involvement in planning
- Community-owned ecotourism operations
- Ecotourism on community-owned land

9. *Promotion, Marketing and Agents*

- Who and where are the ecotourists?
- What do they want?
- How do we reach them?
- What will they pay?
- How do we convince them to buy?

10. *Ecotourism and Development Planning*

- Ecotourism *cf.* other land uses
- Relative sustainability and profitability
- Infrastructure requirements
- Multi land-use options

11. *Ecotourism and Governments*

- National ecotourism plans and strategies
- Links between government portfolios and industry sectors
- Infrastructure planning
- Integrated marketing

12. *The Future of Ecotourism*

- Integration with adventure lifestyle sectors
- Amenity migration and real estate development
- Long-term economic significance

2.11 Suggestions by the Participants for Ecotourism Curriculum

1. Certificate course
2. 3 – 4 months duration
3. 60 per cent field and 40 per cent class session

4. Focus—success ecotourism models
5. Essential for Hoteliers, Forest department, Tourism Department and other stakeholders
6. Dialogue—communication with the department
7. Use of media for marketing
8. Community Based Ecotourism may be a specialisation in the course
9. In addition to these topics like Psychology of tourists and food management has to be taught in the course.

RESOLUTIONS OF FOREST OFFICERS

The participants were requested to resolve about the actions that they would initiate after going back to their work place. The resolutions are quoted

- Tapping of local talents in the area of culture and ethnic values of the region.
- Clustering of resources to prevent overcrowding.
- Will build linkage among the stakeholders.
- Capacity building of forester, villagers and tourists.
- Interpretation centres and extension-value education.
- Talk to local communities on the potentialities/ecotourism as an alternative to consumptive use of resource base.
- Talk to tourists about ecotourism.
- Attributes of an area.
- Susceptibility of the area to pollution.
- On garbage disposal.
- Responsibilities expected of them.
- Talk to the staff.
- To convince the staff of the potentiality of the area.
- How their jobs will be easier if the community is involved in ecotourism enterprise.
- Impart them skills as required.
- Talk to the HOD and controlling officer.
- Talk to the hoteliers/tour operators.
- Draw an ecotourism management plan.

- Will prepare a report on ecotourism potential in the state.
- Tell the importance of the ecotourism to all field level officers.
- Will prepare an ecotourism plan for PAs/sanctuaries and other areas with ecotourism potential.
- Influence the policy makers to evolve ecotourism policy for the state.

2.12 Expectations of the Participants from the Training Programme/Workshop

- Good course input.
- Training programme will add to our knowledge and experiences.
- To know something new about ecotourism.
- Training on a much talked about subject.
- To interact with colleagues from other States.
- To know ecotourism in totality.
- Fruitful interaction and up-to-date information.
- To know more about the concept of ecotourism and preparation of such plan for socio-economic development.
- To understand the concept, scope, potential and practice of ecotourism.
- To understand and appreciate the concept of ecotourism and explore, the possibility of exploring in the state.
- To become aware of the strategies of sustainable development through ecotourism.
- To be acquainted with ecotourism policies and success stories.
- To have details of subjects linked with management of forest and wildlife.
- To know about the work done in various areas in ecotourism and techniques of improving it.
- To familiarise with ecotourism concepts, policies and its practical approach.
- To share experiences and know more about ecotourism.
- To know what other forest department are doing in the field of ecotourism.

- To learn the concept of ecotourism.
- To get a lot of exposure and awareness about ecotourism.
- To know about tourism in forest areas.
- To get the real meaning of ecotourism and livelihood.
- To understanding the modalities if community participation in ecotourism.
- To undergo training programme for promoting nature sites.
- To understand the importance of ecotourism for livelihood.

2.13 Suggestions for Improvement of Training Programme

1. People working in successful models of ecotourism to be invited for experience sharing.
2. Discussion should be held on the psychology of tourist and their inspirations.
3. Experts in the field of ecotourism should be invited for discussion.
4. More case studies of successful ventures of ecotourism to be included.
5. Apart from forest, the area around the city should be included under the study for ecotourism.
6. Additional topics to be discussed:
    - Ecotourism through ecodevelopment committees.
    - Marketing strategies for ecotourism projects.
    - Environmental impact assessment for ecotourism.
7. More analytical case studies needed. Panel discussion should be more focused with a good moderator.
8. Short course on ecotourism should be made compulsory for all IFS officers.
9. Good resource persons should be invited to deliberate on the subjects.
10. Course to be supplemented by case studies.
11. Focus should be given on the both positive and negative aspects of ecotourism.
12. Comprehensive deliberation on the subject is necessary before the forest officials.

PAPERS PRESENTED

3

ECOTOURISM—LIVELIHOOD SECURITY— BIODIVERSITY CONSERVATION INTEGRATION

A HOLISTIC APPROACH

A.K. BHATTACHARYA AND YOGESH DUBEY

Background

India is among one of the twelve mega bio-diversity countries with vast resources in the form of natural landscapes and bio-diversity areas and heritage sites. These areas provide tremendous potential in terms of promoting ecotourism. In most of the areas we are faced with at least two major issues in making ecotourism a practicable tool for sustainable development. One issue is how to develop and manage the 'know-how' for ecotourism without posing threat to the bio-diversity. The other issue is how to integrate ecotourism with the biological and the sociological environments. To develop ecotourism as a tool for such areas it is important that it be developed and managed in a manner whereby all threats to global bio-diversity are minimised and options for sustainable livelihoods are being created. With human pressures all around, bio-diversity conservation is also a question of providing sustainable livelihoods where ecotourism is a good opportunity for community involvement for outsourcing their livelihoods and a way for bio-diversity conservation. The present understanding amongst the forest policy makers, managers and tour operators about the complexities of ecotourism is not exhaustive and hence it calls for better understanding and efforts to be made in this direction.

The three basic challenges generally faced in this area relate to bio-diversity conservation, promotion of community development and management of ecotourism as a viable alternative. Given the status of threatened ecosystems in India, ecotourism needs to be managed in such a way that the integral values and functions of bio-diversity conservation areas are maintained and enriched and also such activities yield reasonable pay offs at the local level.

Tourism to Ecotourism

Ecotourism is a component of the field of sustainable tourism. Ecotourism aspires in all cases to achieve sustainable development results. However, it is important to stress that all tourism activities, be they geared to holidays, business, conferences, congresses or fairs, health, adventure or ecotourism, should aim to be sustainable. This means that the planning and development of tourism infrastructure, its subsequent operation, and its marketing should focus on environmental, social, cultural and economic sustainability criteria.

The following basic components are common and integral in all the available definitions of ecotourism:

- Nature Based Tourism
- Ecological Sustainable Management (Long Term Conservation of Resources)
- Conservation education and interpretation of natural Environment
- Local Community Participation and Benefits
- Tourists' satisfaction

The strong orientation of the ecotourism field towards principles, guidelines, and certification based on sustainability standards gives it an unusual position in the tourism field. In the years since the concept was first defined, a general consensus has formed on the basic elements of ecotourism.

Eco-tourism

- Contributes to conservation of bio-diversity.
- Sustains the well-being of local people.

- Includes an interpretation/learning experience.
- Involves responsible action on the part of tourists and the tourism industry.
- Is delivered primarily to small groups by small-scale businesses.
- Requires the lowest possible consumption of non-renewable resources.
- Stresses local participation, ownership and business opportunities, particularly for rural people.

Ecotourism is of special interest for its relationship with conservation, sustainability, and biological diversity. As a development tool, ecotourism can advance the three basic goals of the Convention on Biological Diversity:

- Conserve biological (and cultural) diversity, by strengthening protected area management systems (public or private) and increasing the value of sound ecosystems;
- Promote the sustainable use of bio-diversity, by generating income, jobs and business opportunities in ecotourism and related business networks; and
- Share the benefits of ecotourism developments equitably with local communities and indigenous people, by obtaining their informed consent and full participation in planning and management of ecotourism businesses.

In the field, well-planned and managed ecotourism has proven to be one of the most effective tools for long-term conservation of bio-diversity when the right circumstances (such as market feasibility, management capacity at local level, and clear and monitored links between ecotourism development and conservation) are present.

Ecotourism Development to Development Oriented Tourism

"Integrated tourism, to be successful, must promote sustainable development by establishing a durable productive base that allows local inhabitants and service providers to enjoy rising standards of living". This was said by Mr. David Barkin in one of his papers in 1996 when the concept of ecotourism was shaping up and words used for "sustainable tourism development" were "integrated tourism". There is no doubt that people consider "ecotourism" as "sustainable tourism". Ecotourism can be used as an effective tool, which ensures ecological, environmental, economical and cultural friendly tourism.

There is no doubt that Tourism has become an important sector for developing countries seeking to maximize foreign exchange earnings, increase employment and secure financial resources to conserve natural and cultural heritage. There is another very important factor in tourism industry, that is its marketing mechanism. Decisions made by tourists and the industry in the originating countries can assist or harm local communities, who are not being involved when tour is being planned, marketed, sold and bought.

Inappropriate tourism development can result in local people losing access to water, land and communal areas, and to the creation of tourist enclaves and to social pollution.

The positive contribution of tourism is significant, but there are a number of challenges to be met if the potential for sustainable local development and poverty elimination, through the localization of benefits, is to be realized. These challenges include issues of ownership, economic leakage (from the local economy and through imports), local employment, benefit distribution, social and environmental impacts and dependency. These problems can only be effectively addressed at the destination level with the active participation of the local communities, tour operators and government agencies.

Rapid and sustained tourism growth and the search for new destinations mean that more and more communities will be affected by the tourism industry. This provides opportunities for economic development, but there are also costs to be minimized. The demand side drives the industry; however, the sustainability of the sector at the destination is dependent upon some public control over the effects of the industry on the environment and socio-cultural structure of the area. It is the natural and cultural heritage of the area and the living culture of the local people that attract tourists. The negative impacts of tourism on the environment and local communities need to be managed and the adverse impacts mitigated in order to maintain the asset.

A tourism monoculture adversely affects the inherent quality of the destination and over-dependence on tourism increases the economic vulnerability of the area to decisions made elsewhere by consumers and investors. Tourism development frequently brings with it demands for goods and services which are not produced in the local economy. These goods and services are then showered outside the local area, often internationally, and only a small proportion of the expenditure remains in the local economy. This is a particular problem in mountain areas. These leakages reduce the development impact of tourism, whereas the development of linkages results in the creation of more jobs and opportunities to locals.

Community based Ecotourism

In its basic concept, community-based ecotourism refers to ecotourism enterprises that are owned and managed by the community. Furthermore, community-based ecotourism implies that a community is taking care of their natural resources in order to gain income through operating a tourism enterprise and using that income to better their lives. It involves conservation, business enterprise and community development. In any community-based ecotourism enterprise there will be direct and indirect participants and direct and indirect beneficiaries. It is important that the entire community has some level of involvement and some level of benefit. Direct participants in a community ecotourism enterprise would be the managing committee and the actual workers involved with producing products or services for sale. In some instances those who are the primary users of a resource might be involved as participants in a project as well. Indirect participants would be the broader community who selected the management committee of a project and those who do not directly use the natural resources involved in an enterprise. Direct beneficiaries would be employees, craft producers, guides, committee members, etc., while indirect beneficiaries would be the wider community as recipients of community development projects funded by tourism revenues would.

Issues to be Aware of when Developing Community-based Ecotourism

The "community-base" for community enterprises is rarely, if ever, all encompassing. Those community members with some initial disadvantages, such as poor housing, insufficient land or income, tend to be among those excluded from participation with ecotourism enterprise development. And, depending on how the ecotourism enterprise is designed, they may be excluded from the benefits of ecotourism development as well as the issue of participation. While there is an increasing recognition of the need to involve communities in general, there is much less agreement about exactly who should participate and to what extent. One common definition states that participation is "giving people more opportunities to participate effectively in development activities...empowering people to mobilize their own capacities, be social actors rather than passive subjects, manage the resources, make decisions and control the activities that affect their lives." How a community chooses to define participation will be important for determining what level of participation will satisfy the ecotourism project goals. It is a very tricky subject. For even where attempts at all inclusive community involvement are well thought out, participation has sometimes been decided on the basis of political affiliation, landownership, kinship or gender.

Linking Communities, Conservation and Development

It has been argued, in a review of integrated conservation and development projects (ICDP) in Latin America, Africa and Asia, that for an ICDP to achieve its bio-diversity conservation goals, it is not enough for the development component to foster improved local living standards—a difficult enough task.

The development process must not only be economically and biologically sustainable, but must also conserve the ecosystem of the protected area. To satisfy this exacting requirement, explicit linkages between project development components and conservation objectives are needed. "Ecotourism" is one concept that has been heralded as a means for establishing such linkages. Unfortunately, while there has been a great deal of discussion about the contributions of ecotourism to local community well-being, very little is visible on the ground. There have been numerous efforts to create "guidelines" for ecotourism development, and the bulk of these assign local participation a privileged position. However, these guidelines have not focused on community-based enterprises nor addressed what, if any, mechanisms exist for nurturing community interest in establishing such enterprises. Rather, they tend to view local participation as something incorporated into the design and implementation of ecotourism enterprises, which are launched from "outside" the community. Additionally, they tend to focus on the quantitative dimensions of participation (e.g. number of people involved, revenue generated) rather than qualitative aspects of local participation (positions in the ecotourism enterprise). Whether a community-based tourism enterprise encourages community conservation of natural resources depends on at least four factors: (i) the scale of benefits received by local residents (and whether they outweigh the short term costs of foregoing resource use or changing resource management); (ii) the extent to which the benefits are clearly perceived as dependent on the resource base and, therefore, on sustainable management; (iii) whether benefits reach all resource users; and (iv) whether local institutions are strengthened, so as to increase their capacity for collective resource management. If the above conditions are not met, massive financial earnings for a few people will not necessarily change communities' approach to resource utilisation. Changes in resource use will also depend on whether communities gain rights/ownership and control over resources and hence a sense of responsibility for their management. Developing mechanisms for local residents to benefit directly from the establishment of ecotourism enterprises in and around their home areas can help offset any loss of revenue from traditional extractive activities, which may be curtailed, in some instances, by the establishment of the new enterprise. It can also motivate community participation in conservation activities if adequate rewards can be consciously realized. Developing National Community Based Ecotourism Strategies can help focus efforts on achieving such mechanisms. At the least, it is a very good way of beginning the process of forging the partnerships deemed so valuable to the process.

Issues and Options

Ecotourism *per se* in India is identified with only Protected Areas. The very concept of Ecotourism should not only be applied to National Parks and Sanctuaries but should also be extended to areas falling outside the Protected Area network. This would include forested areas outside the PA Network. The need of the day to explore the possibilities of ecotourism potential in other areas which contain natural character. By doing this we would also be able to overcome the problems related to carrying capacity by evenly or rather distributing the tourism pressure effectively to other areas. The potential to develop the forest fringe areas into recreational sites should also be considered. These areas could be developed for special category of tourists whose prime interest is recreation.

Policy Issues

The national policy on tourism stipulates that tourism should become a unifying force nationally and internationally fostering better understanding through travel. The national policy on ecotourism also emphasises the need of involvement of local communities for overall development of the area. It also aims at identifying the conflicts between resource use for tourism and the livelihood of local people and attempts to minimize them. The significance of tourism development and its compatibility with environment and socio-cultural characteristics has also been emphasised. Keeping the present framework of policy directives on ecotourism achieving the goals does not look like a Herculean task. Under the present scenario it is important to do a complete need analysis as to what is required in which all areas considered to have potential of ecotourism. How and what kind of mechanisms could be used for involvement of community? Ecotourism in the forest areas is generally being regulated by Forest departments of the respective States but it is still not a recognized programme of the Forest Department. Forest Departments of respective States should take up the Ecotourism as a major programme and develop policy guidelines in concurrence with the existing National and State level policies. There is also a need to bring in little more element of liberalisation in terms of making policy little flexible to attract more investors in this area.

Strategies for Sustainable Ecotourism

Tourism is one of the most important industries of the world and contributes substantially to the economies of all the countries, with an annual turnover worth US$ 350 billion and employs 11 per cent of the total workforce of the world (PATA). Even in India, which gets a very small proportion of world's foreign tourist, tourism is the third largest foreign exchange earning activity. However, the share of nature based tourism is very small in the overall earning whereas many of the east African economies are thriving on the nature based tourism industry.

There are many reasons why National Parks and landscapes in India are not the destinations of tourists. One of the main reasons is that most of our nature conservation areas do not have ecotourism development as one of their prime objectives of management as it is considered to interfere with the conservation objectives of these areas.

Therefore, it is extremely important to evolve a strategy by which ecotoursim could be established as an industry on sustained basis. The strategies could be broadly classified into two categories, namely short term strategies and long term strategies.

Short Term Strategy

The first and the foremost to begin with would be to identify potential areas and prepare a detailed inventory of such areas in terms of their tourism potential. The local communities residing in such areas should be taken into confidence right from the beginning and their involvement should be clearly defined. The local communities should be amply motivated so as to sustain their interests in a particular area where ecotourism is to be planned. Ecotourism planning should be directly linked with the livelihood issue and options that would be generated in any area for the local people. Organizing workshops for local communities to explain them the rationale of ecotourism and how it is going to better their lives could be part of immediate strategy. These workshops could also be coupled with launch of awareness programme in such areas. Village level committees could be formed if the motivation levels are found to be satisfactorily high.

Long Term Strategies

Re-examination of the existing regulations and development of new policy should be done to make Ecotourism more business friendly without affecting the conservation of forest and wildlife. Research and monitoring should be promoted in such areas to find newer possibilities of enhancing and developing tools for effective ecotourism. Research should also be promoted in these areas to develop best practice guides for regions, which have similar kind of, forest areas and biological diversity. Strategies should be developed so as to ensure the original ecological character of the area on long term basis. Tourism packages should be developed so that they are economically viable and are attractive enough to draw tourists to such areas. A lot needs to be done in terms of infrastructure development. Good interpretation centres should be developed with good audio visual aids so as to give a synoptic understanding of the area where a tourist is interested to visit. It would also be extremely important to build linkages between various agencies related to the tourism and centralized information centres being created from where information could be easily accessed. A more robust and strong marketing strategy needs to be developed so as to make all the potential areas of tourism visible to the national and international community.

4

ECOTOURISM PLANNING

A.K. BHATTACHARYA

Tourism

Tourism is the temporary movement of people to destinations outside the normal place of work and residence, the activities undertaken during their stay in those destinations and the facilities created to cater to their needs.

- Ideological difference amongst tourists
- Value system vary amongst tourists
- Increasing numbers concerned about the harm they can do to
  - Ecology
  - Wilderness
  - Local people
- Tourism is the fast growing social and economic phenomena of the twentieth/twenty-first century
- Increased awareness of environment, cultures, histories
- Increased availability of surplus income

Ecotourism

- Ecotourism is a responsible travel to natural areas which conserve the environment and improves the welfare of local people
  - Kenya $ 500 million/year or 10 per cent of GDP
- Ecotourism should
  - Create and satisfy hunger for nature

- Sell nature to conserve
- Use local resource and local expertise
- Educate
- 1980s Environmental Opportunism: A marketing Tactic?

Ecotourism is being considered as a potential strategy to support the conservation of Natural resources whilst at the same time promoting local sustainable development.

Ideally ecotourism involves :

- Conservation
- Development
- Education
- Local control
- Biocentricism
- Symbiotically related

Types of Ecotourism

- Active Ecotourism
- Passive Ecotourism
- Ethical Ecotourism

Typology of nature tourism

Type	*Characteristics*
Casual	Incorporated into tour itineraries
Main stream Nature tourist	Elite, status conscious groups on expensive unusual tours: Local conditioned tailored so can "rough it" in conflict
Dedicated nature tourist	Make trips specifically to see protected areas Local conditions are part of the experience
Hard core nature tourist	Researchers or specialist education groups Local conditions essential part of experience

Different Forms of Tourism

Niche Types of Tourist Markets

- ***Special Interest Tourism***
  - Nature/Cultural/Historic/Local Environment
- ***Adventure Tourism***
  - 'White Water' Boating through River Rapids/Hiking/Trekking/Rock and Mountain Climbing/Fishing/Wildlife Viewing/Scuba Diving
- ***Village Tourism***
  - Local Life Style/Traditional Villages/Village Activities/Traditional Art and Crafts
- ***Farm, Ranch and Plantation Tourism (Rural Tourism)***
  - Farm/Ranch/Plantation House
- ***River and Canal Tourism***
  - Boating on Local Rivers/Canals
- ***Cruise Ship and Yachting Tourism***
  - Large Lakes/Seas/Oceans
- ***Road Touring Tourism***
  - Countryside Motels/Dhabas alongside Roads
- ***Railway Touring Tourism***
  - Tours on Historic Trains
- ***Camping and Caravan Tourism***
  - Camp Grounds/Caravan Parks/Landscaping
- ***Residential Tourism***
  - Planned Resorts/Retirement Home
- ***'Roots' and Nostalgic Tourism***
  - Ancestral Home Areas
- ***Religious Tourism/Pilgrimage Tourism***
  - Religious Sites
- ***Youth Tourism***
  - Learning and Recreation Experiences
- ***Elder Hostel***
  - Senior Citizen/Third Age/Educational Programmes
- ***Cultural Exchange, Study Tours and Home Visit Programmes***
  - Individual or Small Groups of Persons of Common Interests to Visit in another Country

Potential benefits through ecotourism

- Generation of funds for protected areas
- Creation of jobs
- Promotion of awareness
- Development of infrastructures
- Potential cost
  - Environmental degradation
  - Economic inequity and instability
  - Negative socio-cultural changes

Ecotourism goals can be achieved

- Through intersectoral involvement of government, private enterprise, local communities and non-government organizations
- Setting up strict guidelines or regulations
- Developing an ecotourism policy
- Developing an ecotourism plan/strategy

Planning

- Planning is predicting or estimating the future conditions and preparing for the same
  - It helps in quicker achievement of objectives
  - It helps enhance the benefits from the project
  - It helps minimize environmental and social costs
- Planning of ecotourism can be taken of
  - National/Regional/State
  - Local/Site level

Regional/State Planning

- Based on National/Regional/State Ecotourism policy
- Inventory of all existing attractions and potential opportunities
- Destination zone/cluster creation
- Determine a desirable tourism situation and identify steps to reach this situation
- Develop an ecotourism strategy document taking into consideration the States development plan

- Develop infrastructures—road, communication, health etc. which are ecologically sound
- Allow development as per strategy document with contributions from private, public and communities
- Develop guidelines for all stakeholders
- Regulate through some enforcement agency, e.g. Park official, Forest Department, Police etc.

Local/Site level

- Assessment of Ecotourism potential
  - Uniqueness of attraction
  - Susceptibility to impacts
  - Diversity of ecotourism activities
  - Compatability of ecotourism to other mass tourism
  - Climate/environmental conditions
- Market
  - Forecasting of demand for nature of products
  - Difficult
  - Uncertainties due to international currency, exchange, political situations, law and order, diversity of destinations etc.
- Travellers image and satisfaction
  - Pre-image
  - Participation and Evaluation
- Consumer behaviour
  - Needs, perception, life styles
  - Environment influences
  - Marketing strategies (product, price, advertising and distribution
- Activities
  - Camping
  - Trekking
  - Wildlife

- Transport/Access
    - Time
    - Mode
- Resort
    - Low cost—eco friendly
    - Blends with environment
    - Local materials and enterprise
    - Clean and well maintained
    - Alternative energy system
    - Proper garbage and waste disposal
    - Uniqueness "part of surroundings"
- Community investment and development
    - Jobs
    - Livelihoods
    - Source of support facilities
    - Economic development of the area
- Natural/forest/wildlife
    - Revenue additions
    - Increased protection
    - Centres of economic development
- Promotion
    - Advertisements
    - Brochures
    - Travel agents
    - Media
    - Internet
- Services
    - Housekeeping
    - Boarding
- Activities
    - Trail hiking
    - Mountain biking
    - Bird watching/wildlife
    - Cultural visits
    - Fishing
- Pricing

Assessment of Ecotourism Potential Sites

- ***Physical***
  - Attractiveness of nature
  - Accessibility
  - Climate
  - Conditions and attractiveness of local infrastructures
  - Physical risk to visitors, health and safety risk
- ***Social and Institutional***
  - Local people's perception of their environmental resources
  - Local people's awareness of what it has to offer potential visitors—environment, cultural
  - Local culture—festivals and customs, livelihoods
  - Ability of communities to make and enforce decision
  - Hierarchy in the community and institutional gaps
  - Local support for ecotourism NGOs
- ***Market and Economic***
  - Local vested interest and potential competitors for resources
  - Complementary attractions and tourism destinations
  - Existing or potential competition
  - Role and power of tour operators
  - Existing or potential market links
  - Access to credit

Ecotourism Planning Principles

- Apply strict conservation measures to the natural area to protect the flora, fauna and ecosystems and any existing archaeological and historic sites.
- Establish carrying capacity standards so that there is not over development of tourist facilities or over use of environment by visitors.
- Develop small scale tourist facilities in environmentally suitable locations, with locally based design, use of local building materials, energy saving devices and proper disposal of waste material. A visitor with exhibits about the site and local conservation techniques should be developed.

- Prepare and distribute ecotourism codes of conduct for tourists and tour operators, and monitor application of these codes.
- Provide well trained guides who will give accurate information to tourists, educate tourists about biological diversity, conservation techniques and observe good conservation measures during tours.
- Integrate local communities into tourism development by providing them jobs and income from tourism, arrange village tours where appropriate and educate tourists about the local cultures including their economic activities and how to show respect for their cultural traditions.

Problems with Ecotourism

- Initial motivations
  - Interest groups
- Tourist motivations
  - Who are the ecotourists
- Transformative value
  - An active learning experience
- Carrying capacity
  - Environmental limits
  - Social limits (An affective experience)
- Relation of local people to their resources
  - Local control
  - Patronizing tribal people
- A Search for Environmental Authenticity
- Communicative Staging
- Ecotourism theory has not been successful in practice
- Has Ecotourism become a sponsored, commercial product
- Eco Centric

5

ENVIRONMENTAL AUDITING IN ECOTOURISM

A.K. Bhattacharya and Bijendra Basnyat

Ecotourism and Ecotourism Auditing (EA)

- EA is described as "means to an end by which environmental considerations are integrated into tourism business decisions
    - *is therefore highly suited to ecotourism.*

Ecotourism

- Significant travel to natural areas to understand culture, natural, history and environment without altering the integrity of the ecosystem, whilst creating economic opportunities that make the conservation of natural resources financially beneficial to local communities.
- Key elements of ecotourism
  —Natural based
  —Involve education
  —Operated on sustainable basis (Conservation).

Integrating EA and Ecotourism

- Pragmatic tool for tourist operations to use with the goal of attaining sustainable development.

- Allows ecotourist operation to reduce environmental impacts.
- Cost efficient and provides suggestions to improve the environmental management.
- Incorporation of EA into ecotourism industry through environmental management standards such as ISO 14000.

Methods of Conducting EA in Ecotourism

- Gathering background information
- Planning the Audit
- Monitoring on compliance of different legislations, follow of management plant etc.
- Interviewing the Site Personnel, Visitors, Hotel operators on their concern towards ecotourism
- Identification of the waste and management
- Assess the number of visitors and its management
- Field Observation
- Synthesis of Data
- Preparing and distribution of draft report
- Determining the potential solution
- Recommendations and actions
- Develop indicators for monitoring ecotourism
  - Group Work
  - Field Study

Objectives

- Examine the existing code of conducts, rules, regulations, circulars and guidelines for ecotourism in the tourism destination area (TDA) and assess strength and weakness as well as its compliance (GROUP A)
- Identify different types of solid waste generated in TDA, assess waste management system and efficacy of it (GROUP B)
- Assess the tourism situation in TDA and assess its impacts on environment (GROUP C)
- To assess the visitor as well as management authority's attitudes about ecotourism, code of conduct and environmental laws, rules, regulations, circulars and guidelines (GROUP D)
- Develop indicators for monitoring of ecotourism (All groups)

Field Work and Presentation

- Field Work—Half day
- Presentation Preparation—Homework
- Presentation —20 min each group
- Discussion—10 min each group
- Brainstorming on indicators proposed

Presentation Outline

- Methodology
- Present Situation
- Management System being Practiced
- Issues/Problem
- Recommendations
  - General
  - Indicators for conducting EA

Rules and Regulations

- Collect different legislation and prepare a brief summary of it
- Analyze the strength and weakness and identify gap and lacunae in legislation
- Assess the compliance in the field through survey, interactions with Park management staff and observation
- Explore reasons for non-compliance, if any
- Suggest for changes and amendment if required
- Suggest methods for effective implementation
- Develop indicators to integrate EA and ecotourism from legislation perspective

Solid Waste Management

— Identify and quantify different types of solid waste generated in TDA from tourism activities, zoo management etc.

— Interact with management authorities and discuss on its current management practices

— Assess the effectiveness of the solid waste management process as well as its environmental impacts

— Assess different types of information system (banner, pamphlets, hoarding etc.) use for educating people
— Identify area of waste minimization and suggest measures for it
— Suggest indicators to integrate EA and ecotourism from solid waste management perspective

Tourism

- Estimate the number of visitors as well as vehicles per day visiting TDA and its impact on environment as well as on wildlife (air, water, noise pollution etc.)
- Identify different types of tourism activity (e.g. walking, drive, boating etc.) in TDA and its impact on environment as well as on wildlife (air, water, noise pollution etc.)
- Identify different types of system followed for educating visitors and analyze its efficacy
- Identify issues and suggest recommendations
- Suggest indicators to integrate EA and ecotourism from tourism perspective

Survey of Attitudes

- Develop a brief checklists for survey to assess awareness about ecotourism, code of conduct, environmental laws, rules, regulations, circulars and guidelines
- Survey at least 20 visitors and available park management authorities
- Analyze data
- Identify issues and suggest recommendations
- Suggest indicators for measuring EA

Brainstorming

- Rapporteur will summarize indicators of each group
- Discussion on each indicators proposed
- Addition and Deletion of Indicators
- New indicators

6

COMMUNITY BASED ECOTOURISM
IDENTIFICATION OF ISSUES AND OPTIONS THROUGH STAKEHOLDERS ANALYSIS

A.K. BHATTACHARYA, SUCHITRA BANERJEE AND VANDANA SAKSENA

Background

Community-based ecotourism refers to ecotourism enterprises that are owned and managed by the community. Furthermore, community-based ecotourism implies that a community is taking care of their natural resources in order to gain income through operating a tourism enterprise and using that income to better their lives. It involves conservation, business enterprise and community development. In any community-based ecotourism enterprise there will be direct and indirect participants and direct and indirect beneficiaries. It is important that the entire community has some level of involvement and some level of benefit. Direct participants in a community ecotourism enterprise would be the managing committee and the actual workers involved with producing products or services for sale. In some instances those who are the primary users of a resource might be involved as participants in a project as well. Indirect participants would be the broader community who selected the management committee of a project and those who do not directly use the natural resources involved in an enterprise. Direct beneficiaries would be employees, craft producers, guides, committee members, etc., while indirect beneficiaries would be the wider community as recipients of community development projects funded by tourism revenues would.

Hypothesis

The analysis is based on the following hypotheses:

- Ecotourism is a rapidly growing industry—market forces will play an important role in the growth of ecotourism.
- Ecotourism is an effective tool for sustainable wildlife management.
- Community based ecotourism is the only long-term solution for ecotourism.
- There is tremendous potential of ecotourism at national, state and local levels.
- Ecotourism can play a significant role in the livelihood security of the local communities.
- Sensitive issues like carrying capacity and policy need immediate attention.

Objectives

The specific objectives of the analysis were set to :

- Identify key emerging issues in community based ecotourism, specially the community benefits.
- Generate options to address the key issues.

Approach

- The whole analysis was accomplished through participatory approach at all levels involving all the stakeholders ensuring active participation of the stakeholders.
- The stakeholders included officials of different levels from Forest, Tourism, Energy and Rural Development Departments, tourist operators, NGOs, Professionals, Scientists and Academicians, Community members, Village level institutions including forest committees and Gram Sabha members.
- The methodology included intensive and extensive discussions, focus group discussions, village and house surveys through schedules, field visits by combined team of major stakeholders followed by brain storming sessions and presentations of results of the analysis and open house discussions in the workshop.

Ecotourism Defined

About thirty available definitions were reviewed and examined. For the purpose of the analysis following few definitions were considered:

- Responsible travel to natural areas that conserve the environment and sustains the well-being of local people.
- Ecotourism is a significant travel to natural areas to understand the cultural and natural history of the environment, taking care not to alter the integrity of the ecosystem.
- Ecotourism generates economic opportunities that make the conservation of natural resources financially beneficial to local communities

Basic Components

The analysis of the definitions and the concepts of ecotourism led to the identification of following integral components of ecotourism :

— Nature-based tourism
— Ecological sustainable management (long term conservation of resources)
— Conservation education and interpretation of natural environment
— Local community participation and benefits
— Tourists' satisfaction

Why Ecotourism

The review of available literature followed by analysis and discussion identified the following key reasons as to why the ecotourism is significant and be adopted as sustainable tourism:

- Avoids negative impacts that can damage or destroy the integrity or character of the natural or cultural environments being visited.
- Educates the travellers on the importance of conservation.
- Directs revenues to the conservation of natural areas and the management of protected areas.
- Brings economic benefits to local communities and directs revenues to local people living adjacent to protected areas.

- Emphasizes the need for planning and sustainable growth of the tourism industry and seeks to ensure that tourism development does not exceed the social and environmental "carrying capacity".
- Retains a high percentage of revenues in the host country by stressing the use of locally owned facilities and services.
- Increasingly relies on infrastructure that has been developed sensitively in harmony with the environment-minimizing use of fossil fuels, conserving local plant and wildlife and blending with natural environment.

Why Community Based Ecotourism

The key factors to consider 'community based ecotourism' as essential for sustainable tourism were identified as follows :

- Communities are an integral part of ecotourism ecosystem. They can help sustain ecosystem.
- Communities are to be affected first by any influences of ecotourism destination areas.
- For sustainable ecotourism involvement of communities in planning and local management is essential.
- Since ecotourism brings many changes at the community level therefore community should have greater voice in development and conservation of their natural resources.

Ecotourism Linked Key Words

All the key words, which the stakeholders considered had some relevance for the community based ecotourism, were captured. The key words have been arranged in alphabetical order.

Further these key words were categorized into five groups viz., Social, Economic, Ecological, Policy and Institution depending upon the perception of the stakeholders for further analysis.

Accountability
Adventure tourism
Basic needs
Benefit sharing
Bringing people close to nature
Bringing tourists to tribal
Capacity building
Carrying capacity

Conservation (bio-diversity)
Conservers' society
Cooperatives
Cost benefit analysis
Cost effectiveness
Culture and traditions
Eco-development
Eco-friendly
Ecological complexes – ecozones
Employment
Empowerment
Environment education
Funding to initiate
Gene pool
Goodwill of local communities
Governance (at all levels)
Health tourism
Income opportunities
Indigenous technical knowledge
Infrastructure development
Linkages—co-ordination of various departments
Local industries
Losses
Maintenance of system
Manpower
Marketing environment
Marketing indigenous products
Monitoring
Natural heritage
Networking (products)
Orientation
People's participation
Privatization
Publicity
Recreation
Rehabilitation
Religious tourism
Replication model
Representation
Research
Revenue
Stakeholders
Sustainability
Sustainable development
Tribal development
Wildlife friendly
Women's participation

The key words were classified under following categories. The social dimension constituted the maximum percentage :

(%)

	Social	*Economic*	*Ecological*	*Policy*	*Institutional*
Absolute	30.00	16.25	22.50	18.75	22.50
Multiple	43.63	23.63	32.72	12.72	32.72

Problems and Solutions

The details of the problems associated with the community based ecotourism and their solutions were identified as follows :

S. No.	*Problems*	*Solution*
1.	Infrastructure—bad roads	Regular maintenance
2.	Funds	Create autonomous body (cooperative society) Government (state or central)
3.	Marketing of ET	Strengthening existing network
4.	Drinking water	Efficient rain water harvesting Rational use of water Augmentation of drinking water schemes
5.	Improper solid waste management	Treatment plant Recycling of waste
6.	Lack of trained man-power for ecotourism	Training in specialized institutions like IIFM
7.	Increase pollution – air, water	Restriction on vehicle movement Catchments area treatment Wetland management Using better operated vehicles in core areas Harnessing/promoting non-conventional energy source Using cable cart Introducing bullock cart
8.	Exceeding carrying capacity	Horse riding Regulating number of tourists Dispersing tourists by developing other spots
9.	Lack of health facility	Creating health resorts to divert tourists Emergency health services, rescue team
10.	Lack of proper security –law and order	Introducing tourist police Regular police patrolling including odd hours Involving local people in law and order
11.	Exploitation of tourists	Displaying rates of all commodities and services at all tourist spots
12.	Exploitation of local inhabitants	Monitoring by police party/local body having local representative Local guides to be made more responsible Awareness generation/education
13.	Threat to ecology rules	Regulatory control through properly laid out Compulsory plantation by tourists Banning shifting cultivation
14.	Soil erosion	To provide free of cost planting material to local villagers Effective soil conservation measures Metalling of roads

S. No.	*Problems*	*Solution*
15.	Forest fire initiated by tourists	Awareness generation Putting hoarding Educating tourists Interpretation of nature/biodiversity by displaying boards Putting up models and watchtowers Creation of safari
16.	High expectations of tourists (disappointed by not seeing wildlife)	Encouraging bird watching, butterfly Habitat management (salt licks and waterholes) increasing forest cover Establishing animal rescue centres Creating mini zoo/aviary
17.	Shortage of tourists	Organise special events/festivals Inviting educational institutions offering package tours Establishing tourist information centres near bus stand, railway stations Promote incentive tourism Create conducive environment

People—From Problem to Solution

In the background of the recognition of the role of the communities in the natural resource management through various policy measures like Joint Forest management, Panchayati Raj Act etc., the perception of the stakeholders was captured about the change in the attitude of the people over the last one decade—people as problem in 1990 to people as solution in 2002.

People (1990)—Problem	*People (2002)—Solution*
Reluctance	Willingness
No legal framework	Framework existing
Lack of awareness	Awareness
Authoritative	Participative
Individual	Institutional
Restricted	Open
Resolution	Involvement
Lack of policy	Policy development
Low stake	High stake
Fun	Tool of management
Exploitation	Involvement

General Recommendations

Following recommendations were made by the stakeholders for the different aspects and issues :

Aspect	*Issues*	*Plan of Action*	*Who will Take Action*
SOCIAL	Proper planning: safeguarding local culture and tradition of the area as per the interest of the community	Education and awareness	All stakeholders/ Concerned Institution/ Influential people in the village/ Local communitylike Panchayat, youth club, Social worker/ Government agencies/ NGO/ State department of Tourism/ Forest Department
	Promotion of local talent	Encouraging local cultural activities	
	Linking local festivals and rituals	Publicity	
	Conflict	Conflict resolution through some committee at the village level	
	Safety (social security of tourist)	Trust building through the committee	
	Promotion of local people's knowledge related with the integrity of the ecosystem	Application of PRA techniques, dissemination of knowledge through village level workshops	
ECONOMIC	Local employment generation	Economic survey Assessment of resource potential Develop backward and forward linkages Capacity building	Government agencies/ Village level institutions/ NGO/Implementing Agency/ Local bodies with support and capacity building by department and Institutions/ Training by Tourism department
	Use of local people, local products and cuisine	Capacity building through training, awareness programmes	

Aspect	Issues	Plan of Action	Who will take Action
	Infrastructural development	Developing basic facilities by government agencies/ local bodies / funding agencies	
	Introduce local food/ restaurant cuisine	Training	
ECOLO-GICAL	Promotion of indigenous species diversity	Enlisting and protection guidelines Identify sensitive species	Government Department / Forest Department / Research Institution / Municipal Corpora-tion/ NGO / Ecodevelopment committee / Pollution control /Panchayat
	Conservation of biodiversity/ environment with particular emphasis on waste and waste water management	*In situ* and *ex situ* conservation measures involving and em-powering FPC Formation of task force	
	Waste disposal management	Installation of proper waste management facilities	
	Protecting conservation of local area and promoting better environment	Formation of "taskforce" at state/ district level Formation of Ecotourism committees in nearby villages	
POLICY	Empowerment of local communities	Develop suitable legislation through state and central level comittees	Govt Agencies/ Community/NGO / Concerned department
	Development of integrated management plan	State government with institution / experts	
	Participatory policy formulation and its implementation mechanism to implement the policy	Stakeholders participation Government system community system corporate system NGO system	
	Logistics	Roads/transports/ lodging/boarding	

Aspect	*Issues*	*Plan of Action*	*Who will take Action*
	Promotion	Marketing, proper media planning, package and theme based, networking	
	Liberalisation and reduction of restriction	Formulation of liberal legislation	
	Cross sectoral/ inter-departmental linkages	Linkage to be established among all concerned institutions and departments / reduction Conflict through coordination committee The process should be faster for better implementation	
	Review and monitoring of tourism policy	Strict legislation with dos and don'ts rules and act	
	Monitoring and evaluation of ecotourism projects	Survey, observation, mapping and accordingly publicity should be made	
	Zonation of tourism activities I.E., virgin, reserved, undisturbed and restricted zone identification		
INSTITUTIONAL	Involvement of local communities	Formation of village Ecotourism committees	NGO / State Government Tourism Department/ Local Villagers/ Local Bodies
	Formation of State level monitoring committee	Follow up of action on policy (State tourism policy)	

Site Specific Recommendations

During the analysis, an adjoining area having the ecotourism potential was visited by the stakeholders. The following recommendations were made for the promotion of the ecotourism in the area.

1. Preparation of Eco-tourism management plan
2. Training of communities
3. Infrastructure development, laying of trails, construction of day-shelter, transport arrangement, interpretation skills (guides etc.)
4. Local handicraft, cuisine, folksongs/music to be encouraged
5. Bigger and open water bodies should only be used for recreational purpose
6. Infrastructure development
7. Basic facilities development
8. Publicity and promotion of the destination
9. Creation of local committees
10. Securities and departmental co-ordination
11. Promotion of local economic earning activities
12. Long-term planning

Strategy for Community Based Ecotourism

The stakeholders made following recommendations for the short term and long term strategies for the community based ecotourism :

Short Term	*Long Term*
Identification of potential areas.	Policy development.
Motivation of community.	Research and monitoring.
Infrastructure development.	Development of good practices.
Attractive income generation packages.	Empowering the people to self-sustain themselves.
Organising workshops for the local community.	Ensuring the ecological character of the area on a long-term basis.
Provide communication facilities.	Designing media campaigns and other effective outreach measures.
Formation of village (local) level committees.	Development of infrastructure.
Local fee (entry fee).	Providing attractive and economic tourist packages.
Basic facilities development.	Infrastructure development.
Training for local youth and inform of internship for tourism guides.	Market promotion ecotourism.
Awareness programme.	Creating Task force.
Co-ordinating committee formation.	Periodical review of the policy.
Case study development.	

7

TOURISM CARRYING CAPACITY OF PROTECTED AREAS IN MADHYA PRADESH

A.K. BHATTACHARYA AND THRIVEEN SANKAR

Introduction

Emergence of tourism as a major industry is one of the most remarkable changes that have taken place in the economic activity of the post-world war era. The industry has grown from being a marginal aspect of national economic life to an important socio-economic asset since late 1970s. As WTO (1999) observes, tourism is the world's largest growth industry with no signs of slowing down in the twenty-first century. It states that the income from international tourism has increased by an average of 9 per cent annually for the past 16 years to reach US $ 423 billion in 1996. Tourism is also the third largest economic activity after oil and motor industries (Batta, 2000). The number of people who travel for pleasure is believed to comprise between two-thirds and three-quarters of all travellers (Elliot, 1991).

The most important definition for tourism has been provided by Hunziger and Krapf (cited in Burkhart and Medlik, 1974) as, "tourism is a sum of relations and phenomena resulting from travel and stay of non-residents, in so far as it does not lead to permanent residence and is not connected with any permanent or temporary earning activity". This is also the definition accepted by Association

Internationale d' Experts Scientifique du Tourisme (AIEST). A holistic definition is given to tourism by Jafari (1977) as "the study of man away from his usual habitat, of the industry which responds to his needs and of the impacts that both he and the industry have on the host's socio-cultural, economic and physical environments".

The definition for tourist by Ogilvie is as "all persons who satisfy two conditions, that they are away from home for any period of less than a year and that while they spend money in the place they visit without earning it". According to OECD (1994), "tourist is a person staying in a locality situated outside his place of residence during a minimum of 24 hours and a maximum of one year". The United Nations sponsored Conference on Travel and Tourism (1963) in Rome defines visitor as "a person visiting a country other than that in which he has his usual place of residence for any reason other than following an occupation remunerated from within the country visited". Leiper (1979) distinguishes between tourists and excursionists as tourists are temporary travellers staying at least 24 hours in the country visited and purpose of their journey can be classified within leisure and business, while excursionists stay less than 24 hours in the country visited.

The separation of work and leisure is a fairly modern phenomenon. In the Middle Ages in Europe, and in more traditional—especially agricultural—societies even today, people have often had more leisure (Pimlott, 1968). An important factor that changed the tourism patterns was the paid holidays of twentieth century corporate culture (Urry, 1990). With the increase in the number of tourists their variety also increased from the package holiday makers and individual travellers to the drifters and explorers looking for adventure (Cohen, 1972; Plog, 1972). Among these new breed of travellers the ecotourists are the most important.

Background

Ecotourism was defined by The Ecotourism Society (TES) as "responsible travel to natural areas that conserves the environment and sustains the well-being of the local people" (Epler Wood, 1996). Its main aims are ecological and socio-cultural integrity, responsibility and sustainability (Cater, 1994). Ecotourism has developed from the traditional nature tourism and sustainable development concepts. It was Krippendorf's seminal book, *The Holiday Makers,* that introduced to tourism the concept of sustainability (Croall, 1995). However, it was not until 1987 that the Brundtland Commission Report (WCED, 1987) began to stimulate increasing concern and initiate change designed to mitigate some of the growing negative impacts of tourism. WCED defines sustainable development as, which involves the use of natural resources in a way that does not degrade them. Thus the concept of sustainable tourism has also arisen from the principles of resource based or asset-led development. Ecotourism development depends on factors like political stability of the area, commitment of host government and community towards ecotourism, degree of promotion by government and tour operators, the amount of controversy associated with the area, the range of accommodation, infrastructure and other facilities available and continued demand for this increasingly popular and politically correct form of tourism [Kallen, (1990), Moore and Carter (1993), Smelding (1993)].

It is evident that not only has tourism grown rapidly worldwide, but many of those concerned about the negative impacts at the destination assume that mass forms of tourism are responsible for these problems (Cooper and Ozdil, 1992). Although the notion that mass tourism is a bad thing is rather simplistic (Cooper and Ozdil, 1992), it has been suggested that controlling the volume of tourism might alleviate the situation (Wheeler, 1990), especially since the tourism is typically found in locations with fragile environments, such as mountains and coasts which are peripheral to the world economy (May, 1991). Increased interest in alternative forms of tourism is perceived as a response to the emphasis laced on the exploitation associated with mass tourism, especially in developing countries (Fennel and Smale, 1992). This search for an alternative form of tourism is not new as writers has codified such tendencies long before also [Christaller (1964), Turner and Ash (1975), Cohen (1972) and Plog (1972)].

Problems due to Tourism

Ecotourism growth was initiated mainly due to the negative impacts of other forms of tourism on environmental, socio-cultural and economic aspects of the area. The problem arises due to the unrestrained arrival of tourists to the destination and uncontrolled development of facilities beyond the level of tolerance of the different aspects of the area.

Negative effects of tourism on the environment

Effects on natural environment : The effects of tourism on natural environment is divided into five parts : effects on fauna and flora, pollution, erosion, depletion of natural resources and visual impacts.

Effects on built environment : The effects of tourism on built environment can be classified into three main classes—architectural facade, change of land use and burden on infrastructure.

Negative impacts on socio-cultural environment

Impact on Tourists : Quality of recreational experience changes.

Impacts on Host population : May lead to reactions like resistance, retreatism, boundary maintenance, revitalisation or adoption.

Rationale of Studying Carrying Capacity

It was in view of all these negative impacts that principles of sustainable tourism was pursued as a means of attaining environmental sustainability. Goodall and Stabler (1996) has identified five principles of sustainable tourism development. These are: it must generate real net benefits to the society; treat environment as a natural capital; act with caution in the absence of conclusive scientific evidence; use resources so that the environmental quality is not discernibly changed and correct any environmental damage stemming from current tourism activity. Hunter (1997) has demarcated four different approaches to attain sustainable tourism, that is tourism imperative, product-led tourism, environment-led tourism and neotenous tourism.

So the concept of sustainable tourism generally involves recognition of negative impacts of recreation and the need to manage them. It is at this juncture that carrying capacity is cited as the framework within which this objective can be achieved (Hunter and Green (1995), Inskeep (1991), McIntyre (1993), O'Reilley (1986), WTO (1993). It is argued that an alternate way to contain the adverse effects of tourism development on the environment is to estimate the carrying capacity of the destinations and then to check the growth of the infrastructure to that limit. Carrying capacity today is a well-established concept in the general field of resource management and in the particular field of tourism and recreation.

Definition of Carrying Capacity

World Tourism Organisation (1993) defines carrying capacity as, the level of visitor use an area can accommodate with high levels of satisfaction of visitors and few impacts on resource. Mathieson and Wall (1982) defines it as maximum number of people who can use a site without an unacceptable decline in the quality of experience gained by visitors. McIntyre (1993) calls carrying capacity as the maximum use of any site without causing negative effects on the resources, reducing visitor satisfaction, or exerting adverse impact on the society, economy and culture of the area. In tourism, it is the physical, biological, social and psychological capacity of a park environment, for example, to support tourist activity without diminishing environmental quality or visitor satisfaction (Lindsay, 1986).

Carrying capacity becomes an effective measure of sustainability because of the following reasons (Chamberlain, 1997): (i) it is a tool in maintaining the balance between development and conservation; (ii) it is a threshold beyond which one should not go without further planning; (iii) it is a benchmark against which one can measure change and the causes of that change; and (iv) it is an early warning system for trouble. Wall (1982) argues that carrying capacity cannot be set as absolute limit, but as a means to identify critical thresholds which need attention and removing the obstacles by applying controls where possible.

Constraints on the capacity of a site or area to "carry" visitor load may be the result of physical scarcity of space, low level of development, topographic limitations, site inaccessibility, infrastructure limitations and social and cultural constraints (Kaplan, 1996).

Types of Carrying Capacity

According to Batta, R.N. (2000), there are three main categories of carrying capacity, viz. Natural carrying capacity, Social carrying capacity and Economic carrying capacity. Here, natural carrying capacity is demarcated into physical carrying capacity and ecological carrying capacity and social carrying capacity is divided into psychological carrying capacity of tourists and that of hosts.

Criteria for the Measurement of Carrying Capacity

There are six main criteria that are identified as criteria for carrying capacity:

Tolerance of host population: Dogan (1989) examines the reaction of the host towards the tourism activities for the estimation of carrying capacity. Ap (1992) also uses attitude of hosts as the criteria for carrying capacity estimation.

Satisfaction of visitors: Kaur (1979) estimates the carrying capacity in terms of the satisfaction that the visitors are deriving from the site. Dann (1979) identifies this as a dynamic factor that is subject to changes in the long duration. Neil *et al.* (1977) notices that repeat visitors often resents the changes that are made in the destination area.

Excessive rate of growth: Dekadt (1979) emphasizes on this aspect while dealing with carrying capacity estimation.

Capacity based on the cost and benefits: According to Batta (2000), focus of the planners on determining the carrying capacity of the area should be to estimate the cost and benefits that are derived from the activity.

Role of Capacity in a system approach: Getz (1982) outlines the estimation of carrying capacity on the basis of systems approach.

Tangible resource limit: As suggested by Batta (2000) this method envisages making inventories of existing resources and identifying obstacles to development and thus preventing the reaching of carrying capacity.

Carrying Capacity Measurement Models

Carrying capacity can be measured using the following frameworks:

Boullon (1985) offered a formula to estimate the tourist capacity of the area using three variables, namely the ecological, material and psychological called as the Rotation Coefficient.

U.S. Department of the Interior and National Park Service of USA developed the framework called as Visitor Experience and Resource Protection (VERP) for the protected areas. In this method, nine elements are integrated to project the framework for the study, method for analysis, prescriptions for the park and an overview of the study.

Another model which is more used and better known is the LAC (Limits of Acceptable Change) (Stankey *et al.*, 1985). It is based on the idea of evaluative standards presented by Shelby and Heberlein (1986).

Carrying capacity thus can be calculated as a function of the quantity of resources of an area (*Q*), the tolerance of its resources to use (*T*), the number of visitors (*N*), the type of use (*U*), the design and management of visitor facilities (*DM*), and the attitude and behaviour of its tourists and managers (*AB*) (Miguel D. Fortes).

Limitations of Carrying Capacity

According to Lindberg *et al.* (1997) the important limitations are:

- Varying definitions and scope given to carrying capacity study by different researchers.
- Subjectivity of the concept of carrying capacity leading to difficulties in management.

- Seasonality plays a very important role in estimation.
- Complications due to change in perceptions of different stakeholders.

Issues and Problems of Carrying Capacity

Conceptual problem

It is technical and multidisciplinary—Carrying capacity is not an inherent, fixed value of the environment. It can be dismissed by unregulated overuse or enhanced by thoughtful management (Hendee *et al.*, 1990).

Including the social dimension in the carrying capacity concept implies that a carrying capacity level must partly result from a sociopolitical process. So absolute carrying capacity levels do not exist in recreation and tourism (Stankey and Manning 1986).

Some technical difficulties are inherent in operationalizing the concept such as :

First the researchers must identify the connection between the actual impact and what kind and amount of use which causes the impact. This is the descriptive part of the process.

The second step is to decide the critical level of the impact. This is the normative part. Carrying capacity decisions must also be based on value judgements. The question is on what kind of values, or on whose values such decision should be based. The host society is not homogeneous in their attitudes and values, neither is the tourist population (Vistad, 1994).

The most difficult part is to agree on who should influence this value judgement process, and then to discuss and agree upon the values that the management of use and protection of a recreational or tourist area should be based.

Problems due to boundary differences

Spatial and temporal dimensions and boundaries in the human environments do not neatly map onto or correspond with the dimensions in the natural environments. This gives rise to numerous problems in making social and environmental trade-offs. Simple one-dimensional point estimates of carrying capacity are neither realistic nor practical. Yet the assimilative capacity of an area is defined by the natural, not human, boundaries.

Carrying capacity must also be considered in a dynamic or temporal context. Expectations concerning time required for system response or achievement of goals is a fundamental difference between the natural and human environments. The natural environment works on an evolutionary time scale; the human environment, on a short-term scale, which is usually oriented towards present generations.

Problems associated with resource use

Many recreational areas are used by several user groups, each of them seeking different and even conflicting experiences. These different groups in the same area are often different in preference and tolerance (Brown and Haas, 1980; Hendee *et al.*, 1990; Vistad, 1994).

All uses of the natural environment will influence and cause some change in this environment.

Impacts on biophysical resources often do not help establish obvious capacity limits. The right management action will, therefore, usually be to concentrate the use on a few sites, trails, etc. instead of stimulating dispersed visitor patterns.

The number of visitors/tourists is often a poor predictor of the total impact from tourism (Hammitt and Cole, 1987; Kuss *et al.*, 1990). Other factors like timing, type of use, distribution, season, attitudes and knowledge among the visitors might be more important than just the number.

Problem with the concept itself

Perhaps the most serious problem is that many people consider the carrying capacity of an area as an inherent value of the resource base, one that could be determined through careful observation and research (Hendee *et al.,* 1990).

REFERENCES

Ap, J., (1992), Residents Perception of Tourism Impact, *Annals of Tourism Research,* Vol.19.

Batta, A., (2000), *Tourism and Environment*, Indus Publishing Company, New Delhi, p.109

Burkhart, A.J., and Medelik, S. (1974), *Tourism: Past, Present and Future*, Heinemann, London.

Cater, E., (1994), Ecotourism in the Third World : Problems and Prospects for Sustainability, Chapter 5 in E. Cater and G. Lowman (eds.), *Ecotourism ; A Sustainable Option?*, Wiley, Chichester.

Chamberlain, K. (1997). *Carrying Capacity*, Tourism Focus No. 8. United Nations Environment Programme Industry and Development, France.

Christaller, W., (1964), Some considerations of Tourism locations in Europe, *Papers and Proceeding of Regional Science Association,* 12, pp. 377-398.

Cohen, E., (1972), Towards a sociology of international tourism, *Social Research*, 39, pp. 164-182.

Cooper, C.P. and Odzil, I., (1992), From mass to responsible tourism—the Turkish Experience, *Tourism Management*, December 13 (4), pp. 377-386.

Croall, J., (1995), *Preserve or Destroy: Tourism and Environment*, Calouste Gulbenkian Foundation, London.

Dann, J., (1978), Tourist Satisfaction: a highly complex variable, *Annals of Tourism Research,* Vol. 5, No. 4.

De Kadt, E., (1979), (edt). *Tourism: Passport to Development*, Oxford University Press, Oxford.

Dogan, H.Z. (1989), Forms of adjustment: Socio-cultural Impacts of Tourism, *Annals of Tourism Research*, Vol. 16, pp. 216-236.

Elliot, J.A. (1994), Travel and Tourism, *The Economist*, 23 March, pp. 3-26

Epler Wood, M., (1996), Evolution of Ecotourism as a Sustainable Development Tool, *Paper presented at the Sixth International Symposium on Society and Natural Resource Management*, Pennsylvania State University, 18-23, May, 1996.

Fennel, D.A. and Smale, B.J.A., (1992), Ecotourism and natural resource protection: Implications of an alternative form of tourism for host nations, *Tourism Recreation Research*, 17(1), pp. 21-32.

Getz, (1983), Capacity to Absorb Tourism: Concepts and Implications for Strategic Planning, *Annals of Tourism Research*, Vol. 10, pp. 239-63.

Hammit, W.E. and Cole, D.N. 1987. Wildland Recreation. *Ecology and Management.* John Wiley and Sons.

Hendee, J.C., Stankey, G.H. and Lucas, R.C., 1990. Wilderness Management. 2nd ed. North American Press, Colorado.

Hunter, C. (1997), Sustainable Tourism as an Adaptive Paradigm, *Annals of Tourism Research*, Vol. 24, No. 4, pp. 850-867.

Hunter, Colin and Howard Green (1995), *Tourism and Environment: A Sustainable Relationship*, Routledge, London.

Inskeep, E. (1991), *Tourism Planning: An Integrated and Sustainable Development Approach,* Van Nostrand Reinhold, New York.

Jafari, J. (1977), Editor's Page, *Annals of Tourism Research*, Vol. 5, Special. No. 6-11.

Kallen, C., (1990), Ecotourism: The Light at the end of the Terminal, *E- Magazine*, July–August, pp. 37-41.

Kaplan, Motti, (1996), Sustainable Tourist Development, *Israel Environment Bulletin,* Spring 1996-5756, Vol. 19, No. 2

Kaur, J. (1979), Re-examining Tourism capacity of Nainital, in K Sinnhuber and F. Jung (edt), *Studies in Geography of Tourism and Recreation*, Vol.2.

Kuss, F.R., Graefe, A.R. and Vaske, J.J. (1990). *Visitor Impact Management: A Review of Research.* Volume 1. National Parks and Conservation Association, Washington, D.C.

Leiper, N. (1979), The Framework of Tourism, *Annals of Tourism Research*, Oct/Dec, 1979.

Lindsay, J. 1986. *Carrying capacity for tourism development in national parks of the United States,* UNEP Industry and Environment. Jan/Feb/March. 8(1): 17-18.

Mathieson, A. and Geoffrey Wall (1982), *Tourism: Economic, Physical and Social Impacts,* Longman, London, p. 38.

May, V., (1991), Tourism, Environment and Development : Values, Sustainability and Stewardship, *Tourism Management*, June, pp. 112-118.

McIntyre, G. (1993), *Sustainable Tourism Development: Guideline for Local Planners,* WTO, Madrid.

Moore, S. and Carter, B., (1993), Ecotourism in the 21st Century, *Tourism Management*, April 14 (2), pp. 123-130.

OECD (1994), *Environmental Indicators—OECD*, Core Set, Paris.

Ogilvie, F.W. (1993), *The Tourist Movement,* Staples Press, London.

O'Reilly, A.M. (1986), Tourism Carrying Capacity: Concepts and Issues, *Tourism Management*, December 1986.

Pimlott, J.A.R., (1968), *Recreations,* Studio Vista, London.

Plog, S.C., (1972), Why destination areas rise and fall in popularity, quoted in P.E. Murphy, (1985), *Tourism: A Community Approach*, Methuen, London.

Shelby, B. and Heberlein, T. A. (1986), *Carrying Capacity in Recreation Settings.* Oregon State University Press, Corvallis, Oregon.

Smelding, S.S.A., (1993), Low Impact Ecotourism—clarion call or reality? – the challenge of Botswana, *The Tourist Revue*, 3, pp. 25-27.

Stankey, G.H., Cole, D.N., Lucas, R.C., Petersen, M.E. and Frissell, S.S. (1985). *The Limits of Acceptable Change (LAC) System for Wilderness Planning*. Gen. Tech. Rep. INT - 176. U.S. Dept. of Agriculture, Forest Service, Intermountain Forest and Range Experiment Station. Ogden, Utah.

Turner, L. and Ash, J., (1975), *The Golden Hordes : International Tourism and Pleasure Periphery*, Constable, London.

URL: *http://wcpa.iucn.org/biome/marine/seasia/wrkspdocs/ENVIRO.DOC*

URL: *www.planning.nps.gov/document/verphandbook.pdf*

Urry, J., (1990), *The Tourist Gaze : Leisure and Travel in Contemporary Societies*, Sage Publications, London.

Vistad, O. I., (1994). *An analysis of outdoor recreation, environmental experience, environmental impact and management in Femundsmarka National Park, with comparisons to Rogen nature reserve and Langfjallet nature reserve.*— Ph.D. dissertation, Dept. of Geography, University of Trondheim, Norway.

WCED, (1987), *Our Common Future*, Oxford University Press, London.

Wheeler, B., (1990), Responsible Tourism, *Tourism Management*, 11(3), pp. 262-263.

WTO (1993), *Sustainable Tourism Development: Guideline for Local Planners*, WTO, Madrid.

WTO (1999), World Tourism Statistics, URL: *www.world-tourism.org*

APPENDIX 1

Framework for Limits of Acceptable Change (LAC) calculation
Identify area issues and concerns
Define and describe opportunity classes
Select indicators of resource and social conditions
Inventory existing resource and social conditions
Specify standards for the resource and social indicators for each opportunity class
Identify alternative opportunity class allocations reflecting area issues and concerns and existing resource and social conditions
Identify management actions for each alternative
Evaluate and select a preferred alternative
Implement actions and monitor conditions

APPENDIX 2

Framework for Visitor Experience and Resource Protection (VERP) method

Element 1: Assemble an Interdisciplinary Project Team
Element 2: Develop a Public Involvement Strategy
Element 3: Develop Statements of Park Purpose, Significance, and Primary Interpretive Themes; Identify Planning Constraints.

Analysis

Element 4: Analyze Park Resources and the Existing Visitor Use.

Prescriptions

Element 5: Describe a Potential Range of Visitor Experiences and Resource Conditions (potential prescriptive zones)
Element 6: Allocate the Potential Zones to Specific Locations in the Park (prescriptive management zoning)

Overview

Element 7: Select Indicators and Specify Standards for Each Zone; Develop a Monitoring Plan

Monitoring and Management Action

Element 8: Monitor Resource and Social Indicators.
Element 9: Take Management Action

8

RECREATION FORESTRY

INNOVATIONS IN ECOTOURISM

H.S. PABLA

What is a Recreation Forest

- **Forest sites with Potential for developing:**
  - Camping
  - Angling
  - Trekking/Hiking
  - Rock Climbing
  - Bird Watching
  - River Rafting/Canoeing
  - Cultural Experiences
  - Wildlife Viewing
  - Nature Photography; and more

Why Recreation Forests?

- Forestry at the Crossroads (Utilisation *vs.* Ecological Security)
- Alternative to Logging
- Wilderness has High Recreation Value
- Assured Ecological Returns
- Complementary to National Parks
- High Returns

National Parks: "Tourism" not an Objective

- Too remote
- Too small for variety of experience
- Too many restrictions
- Popular destinations over-crowded

Tourism : Some Facts

Contribution	*World*	*India/South Asia*
Turnover	US$ 350 billion	
Workforce	11% of total	2.9 crore
New Jobs by 2007	10 crore	2 crore
Growth Rate		8%
Jobs/lakh		47.5%
Foreign Exchange Earning		1.2% of GDP (3rd highest)
India's Share :		
Arrivals		0.39%
Receipts		0.70%

Where

- Near an Existing Popular Destination
- Access to an Airport
- In Areas with Reasonable Infrastructure
- In Each District (for Locals)

Potential Sites : Madhya Pradesh and Chhattisgarh (Indicative)

1. Khajuraho-Panna
2. Gwalior-Chambal
3. JBP-Kanha-Bandhavgarh
4. JBP-Seoni-NGP
5. Sanchi-Bhopal-Pachmarhi
6. Indore-Mandu
7. Raipur-Bastar

Potential Clients

- Foreigners
- Urban Indians
- Adventure Tourists
- Nature Lovers
- Students
- Scientists

Services

- Recreation
- Education

The Proposal

- Develop Policy
- Identify Potential Sites
- Management Plan Preparation and Approval
- Invite Private Investors for Participation
- Develop Quality Ecotourism Facilities
- Involve Communities
- Share Revenue

Tentative Terms

- MoU for 15-20 years; notice period 1-3 years
- Profit sharing with government/communities
- Lodges may be on non-forest land
- Design, Construction ecofriendly
- Relatively unrestricted use of the area (within the agreed management plan)
- Professional guides and naturalists
- No wood fuel to be used
- Recycling of garbage
- Impact monitoring and mitigation

- Local community interests to be protected
- Site specific

Concerns

- Rights of Communities (grazing, collection of forest produce)
- Environmental Degradation
- Cultural Issues

Possible Solutions

- Involve and Compensate Communities
- Build Safeguards in the MoU
- Awareness and Regulation

Benefits to the State

- Conservation of Natural Resources
- Revenue
- New Employment Avenues
- New Investments
- Public Support to Biodiversity Conservation
- Projection of a Positive Image

Benefits to Communities

- New Employment Avenues
- Direct Income
- Small Businesses
- Development of Remote Areas

Benefit to Investors

- New Business Avenues

9

COMMUNITY BASED ECOTOURISM

A CASE STUDY OF KERWA VAN VIHAR NATIONAL PARK CATCHMENTS, BHOPAL (MADHYA PRADESH)

A.K. BHATTACHARYA, SUCHITRA BANERJEE AND VANDANA SAKSENA

Summary

Ecotourism is growing fast. For sustainable ecotourism management proper planning through the involvement of the local people of the tourism destination areas is considered essential. This chapter attempts to address the various issues of community based ecotourism of a local tourism destination area near Bhopal, the capital of Madhya Pradesh. The perception of the visitors and the local villagers have been captured and analysed, conclusions drawn from the survey and strategy suggested.

Source : Published in Tourism Recreation Research, Vol 28 (1), 2003

Background

From Tourism to Ecotourism

Tourism in general has already become the most important civil industry in the world. According to World Travel and Tourism Council tourism is now the world's largest industry (Lindberg and Hawkins, 1999). Ecotourism is the most important segments of tourism (WTO, 1984 and 1991). The concept of ecotourism evolved in 1980s and this concept mainly developed in response to calls for sustainable forms of tourism. One of these was an increase in environmental consciousness, which had begun in late 1960s and gained momentum in 1980s (Figgis, 1993; Wight, 1993; Figgis, 1994; Harris and Leiper, 1995; Eagles, 1996; Ceballos-Lascurian, 1996).

When the term *ecotourism* first appeared in the 1980s, it was loosely applied towards travel that included any aspect of nature. Most of these travel packages and destinations, however, were little more than mass tourism taken outdoors. Most imparted more impacts than benefits on local communities and habitats. Over the years, changing attitudes by travellers, tour operators, communities and conservationists have significantly narrowed the ecotourism focus.

Butler writes that whale watching that began in response to their depletion of the Humpback whale, Blue whale in the 1960s (resulting in them being declared protected in 1967 and 1966 consecutively) marked the birth of the ecotourism (Cebalos-Lascurian, 1996).

As a result of the increased environmental awareness, eco-development arose as a model that sought to integrate cultural, social and ecological goals with development. It has been suggested that out of this popular school of thought, the concept of ecotourism was developed as an opportunity to put the ideas of eco-development into practice (Sagasti and Colby, 1993; Nelson 1994). Ecotourism, being promoted as a means of 'giving nature value' and hence of achieving sustainable tourism development could be a useful choice besides the other types of tourism (Kamra, 2001).

Ecotourism has been defined in different ways. Ecotourism was first defined by Ceballos-Lascurian as: "Travelling to relatively undisturbed or uncontaminated natural areas with the specific objective of studying, admiring, and enjoying the scenery and its wild plants, as well as any existing cultural manifestations (both past and present) found in these areas" (Commonwealth Department of Tourism, 1994).

The International Ecotourism Society defines Ecotourism as

"Responsible travel to natural areas which conserves the environment and improves the welfare of local people."

A general consensus has formed on the basic elements of ecotourism:

- Contributes to conservation of biodiversity.
- Sustains the well-being of local people.
- Includes an interpretation/learning experience.
- Involves responsible action on the part of tourists and the tourism industry.
- Is delivered primarily to small groups by small-scale businesses.
- Requires the lowest possible consumption of nonrenewable resources.
- Stresses local participation, ownership and business opportunities, particularly for rural people.

Community Based Ecotourim (CBE)

CBE management refers to ecotourism programmes, which take place under the control and active participation of the local people who inhabit or own a natural attraction (Lindberg *et al.,* 1999). CBE works closely with local people, provides incentive for conservation, and more and more often, works outside parks in locally owned land. Communities are an integral part of ecotourism ecosystem. They can help sustain ecosystem. Communities are to be affected first by any influences of ecotourism destination areas. For sustainable ecotourism involvement of communities in planning and local management is essential (Coltman, 1989; WTO, 1993; Cater and Lowman, 1994).

Since ecotourism brings many changes at the community level, therefore, community should have greater voice in development and conservation of their natural resources. Ecotourism can play a significant role in livelihood security as integral parts of ecosystem. CBE implies that a community is taking care of their natural resources in order to gain income through operating a tourism enterprise and using that income to better their lives. It involves conservation, business enterprise and community development. Community managed tourism attempts to let communities decide what type of growth they would like to see and then help them implement their plans (Lindberg and Hawkins, 1999).

Planning for CBE

Ecotourism areas often include existing communities, specially of traditional people, and therefore, ecotourism plan must be holistic in approach and consider ways to conserve local cultural traditions and identities and how to bring benefits to these communities. Although the researches indicate that the CBE can be a powerful force for conservation by providing benefits to local people, but meeting such conservation objectives requires careful and proper planning and design (Lindberg and Hawkins, 1999).

Some planning principles for ecotourism are as follows (WTO, 1998):

- Apply strict conservation measures to the natural areas to protect the flora, fauna and ecosystems and make existing archaeological remains of historic sites.
- Establish carrying capacity standards so that there is no over-development of the tourist facilities or over-use of the environment by the visitors.
- Develop small scale tourist facilities in environmentally suitable locations, with locally based design, use of local building materials, energy saving devices and proper disposal of waste material. A visitor centre with exhibits about the site and local conservation techniques should be developed.
- Prepare and distribute ecotourism codes of conduct for the tourists and tour operators, and monitor applications of these codes.
- Provide well-trained tour guides who will give accurate information to tourists, educate tourists about biological diversity, conservation techniques and observe good conservation measures during tours.

- Integrate local communities into tourism development by providing them jobs and income from tourism, arrange village tours where appropriate and educate tourists about the local cultures including their economic activities and how to show respect for their cultural traditions.

The Study Area—Kerwa Van Vihar National Park Catchments

Kerwa

India in general and Madhya Pradesh in particular having unlimited potential in Ecotourism should be geared up to reap the benefits in a new perspective. One of the essential ingredients of ecotourism is community participation and community benefits. Since the destination areas for ecotourism in Madhya Pradesh are already under tremendous biotic pressure, for sustainable ecotourism, it becomes essential that the local communities are actively involved in its management. So close to the concrete jungle of Bhopal the Kerwa jungles are endowed with scenic and aesthetic values, which attract around one lakh visitors annually. The interesting issue is that most of them are local tourists including villagers from adjoining villages.

The area is close to Van Vihar National Park and has tremendous tourism potential and has also an impact on the socio-economic condition of the villagers. The local communities can play a significant role in the development of ecologically and sustainable management of ecotourism module in the area, on the other hand the ecotourism in the area can play an effective role in the economic development of the villages in the ecotourism destination area. Total available area is 50 sq km whereas Ecotourism impact area is 10 sq km. The common salient features of the area are as follows :

- Local—It is hardly thirteen kms from the main centres of the capital.
- Forests + wildlife—The area is naturally endowed with forests and wildlife.

- Water body—There is a dam, perennial water stream and also some waterbodies.
- Nearest nature—So close to the city the area provides a serene natural surroundings.
- Topography—The area has good landscape, suitable for trekking and aesthetic value.
- Wilderness—The area also provides wilderness for nature lovers.

Van Vihar

Van Vihar, the smallest National Park of India and one of most unique in the world is situated in Bhopal, the capital of largest State of India. Bhopal lies in the eastern edge of Malwa plateau and situated in the central part of State bounded by Rajgarh district in the north-east, Guna district in the east and south-east and Sehore district in the west and south-west.

Nature has tremendous capacity to resurrect itself. Van Vihar National Park is a living example that reflects this capacity of Nature. Van Vihar National Park was established in 1983. A 445 hectares of degraded and denuded hillock adjoining the city and dotted with numerous villages on the other side was provided legal protection by declaring it a National Park on 26th January, 1983.

Both Van Vihar and Kerwa are situated close by, the former being the zoo having the status of national park whereas the latter falls in the revenue forests, part of which has been transferred to the Forest Department for protection.

The Study

Looking to the growing tourism in this area, a tourism potential survey was done to understand the perception of the various stakeholders for planning sustainable CBE in the area.

Objectives

With the hypothesis that the small towns and the rural areas have considerable potential for ecotourism (Gunn, 1988), the specific objectives of the study were set to :

- Identify key emerging issues in CBE, specially the community benefits.
- Generate options to address the key issues.

The study was intended for the following outcomes:

- Approaches for short term and long term strategy for CBE.
- Suggested module for CBE for operationalisation—Kerwa as a pilot project.
- Recommendations for State ecotourism policy guidelines.

Approach

- The whole analysis was accomplished through participatory approach at all levels involving all the stakeholders ensuring active participation of the stakeholders.
- The stakeholders included officials of different levels from Forest, Tourism, Energy and Rural Developments, tourist operators, NGOs, Professionals, Scientists and Academicians, Community members, Village level institutions including forest committees and Gram Sabha members.
- The methodology included intensive and extensive discussions, focus group discussions, village and house survey through schedules, field visits by combined team of major stakeholders followed by brain storming sessions and presentations of results of the analysis and open house discussions in the workshop.

The study was conducted during the period of October 2000 to March 2002. The field surveys were carried out in all the seasons. The responses were received from :

- 69 groups (approximately 500 individuals)—visitors invariably come in groups of 6 to ten.
- 40 households—households were selected through random selection.

However the questions were addressed to the heads of the groups/households, but attempts were made to obtain the group response through participatory approach. Finally, the findings were discussed in a workshop participated by the major stakeholders.

Tourist Perception

Tourist Influx

Tourist in flux data indicate that rainy season is the peak period when the number of visitors visiting Kerwa is the maximum, specially on Sundays and general holidays.

This is followed by winter and minimum influx is in summer.

Seasons	*Average Sunday (annual)*	*Per day other holidays (annual)*
Rains (July/August)	200 (16000)	1000 (8000)
Summer (May/June)	500 (4000)	125 (1000)
Rest of Months	1200 (38400)	600 (19600)
Average	1217	596
Total	58400	28600
Annual Total		*87000*

Visitors Profile

Nearly 79 per cent of the people visiting Kerwa are local visitors coming from different parts of Bhopal while 21 per cent are outsiders.

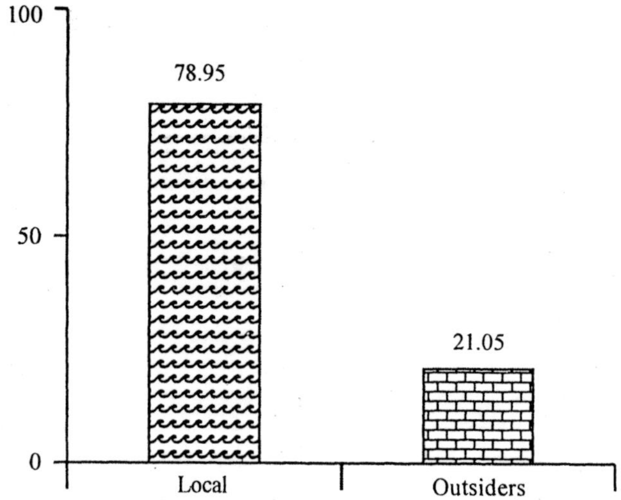

Education Level of Tourists

Most of the people visiting Kerwa are educated. The result of the survey indicates that 37.04 per cent group heads are postgraduates while the percentage of graduates is 33.33 per cent, followed by 18.52 per cent matriculates and 11.11 per cent technical.

Education	%
High school	18.52
Graduate	33.33
Post graduate	37.04
Technical	11.11

Occupation

The survey revealed that around 85 per cent group heads belonged to the service class, of which 15 per cent were from technical field while the rest were non-technical. Of the remaining fifteen per cent, 11 per cent are from business community and 4 per cent of visitors from the students community.

Income Groups

Most of the people visiting Kerwa belong to the middle class having the monthly income ranging between Rs. 3,000 and Rs. 10,000, followed by 26 per cent between Rs. 10,000 and Rs. 15,000. The percentage of visitors whose income lies between 15,001-20,000 is 19 per cent, while that of between 1,500-3,000 is 15 per cent. A very small percentage of people visiting Kerwa is from the high income group.

Income group (Rs.)	%
1500-3000	14.81
3001-10000	37.03
10001-15000	25.92
15001-20000	18.24
> 20000	4.0

Purpose of Visit

The majority of visitors visit the area for recreation. The number of nature loving visitors is also quite good. However, from the discussion it emerged that the dividing line in the perception of the picnic, outing, and love for nature was quite thin.

Purpose of visit	%
Close by picnic spot	57.8
Love for nature	17.5
Outing	15.7
Picnic spot and love for nature	3.5
Picnic spot and love for nature and outing	2.0
All purpose	3.5

Frequency of Visits Per Month

About 91 per cent people visit Kerwa between 1-5 times a month. About 6 per cent people visit 6-10 times a month. Only a small percentage visit it for more than 15 times in a month.

Frequency	*%*
1-5	91.3
6-10	5.20
11-15	1.75
> 15	1.75

Other Adjoining Places being Visited

Besides Kerwa there are some other places also in and around Bhopal, which are of tourists attractions. These places are Kolar Dam, Bhojpur, Bhimbetika, Halali Dam, Lakeview, Kalia Sot Dam, Manbhavan ki Tekri (the highest peak of Bhopal), Delabadi (wildlife area), Lalghati, Chiklod, Raisen Fort and Indira Gandhi Dam. Percentage of the visitors who also visit these areas regularly are as follows :

Sl. No.	*Name of Place*	*Percentage*
1.	Kolar Dam	40.7
2.	Bhojpur	33.3
3.	Bhimbetika	25.9
4.	Halali Dam	25.9
5.	Lake View	14.8
6.	Kalia Sot Dam	14.8
7.	Manbhawan Ki Tekri	7.4
8.	Delabadi	7.4
9.	Lalghati	3.7
10.	Chiklod	3.7

Willingness to Stay if Facilities Provided

Many of the visitors showed interest in staying in the area subject to the availability of proper amenities such as safe drinking water, better roads, trekking, rock gliding, lodging, park, restaurant, medical facilities, fuel, etc. They are ready to pay for these facilities.

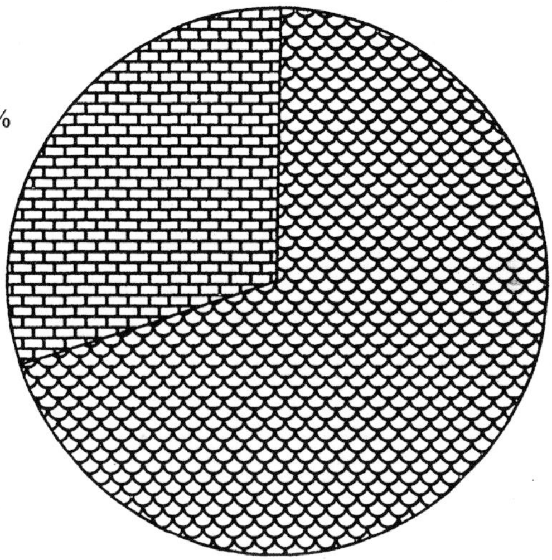

Number of Days Likely to be Spent

Majority (61%) of the tourists are willing to stay up to three days if adequate facilities are provided.

Days	%
1	14.11
2	33.33
3	13.11
4	0
5	0
> 5	12.8
Did not respond	26.65

Facilities Required

The facilities desired mainly include safe drinking water and access.

Facilities	%
Water	18.5
Road	8.2
Trekking	7.0
Rock gliding	6.6
Loding	9.4
Park	7.8
Restaurant	7.4
Medical facility	7.4
Fuel facility	3.7
Did not respond	24.00

Willing to Pay for Stay

Majority of the tourists agree to pay up to Rs 200 per person per day for the necessary facilities.

Payments	%
50-100	22.22
101-200	14.81
201-300	0
301-400	7.41
401-500	0
> 500	3.70
Did not respond	51.86

Problems and Difficulties

Visitors complained for non-availability of safe drinking water, poor public transport, and non-availability of proper shops of essential commodities. Also no trained guide is available for proper guidance about the area. There is no arrangement to check the visitors taking a dip or a swim in the dam for pleasure and fun, as a result there is always a fear of accident. Every year there are reports of few casualties. Besides, the visitors also face the problem of proper toilets and health care facilities.

Problems	*Percentage*
Water	64.9
Transport	22.8
Shop	8.7
Security	5.26
Guides	5.26
Shades	5.26
Others	5.26
Medical facility	3.5
Toilet facility	3.5

Willingness to Stay with Villagers

A large percentage of visitors (74%) are ready to stay with villagers.

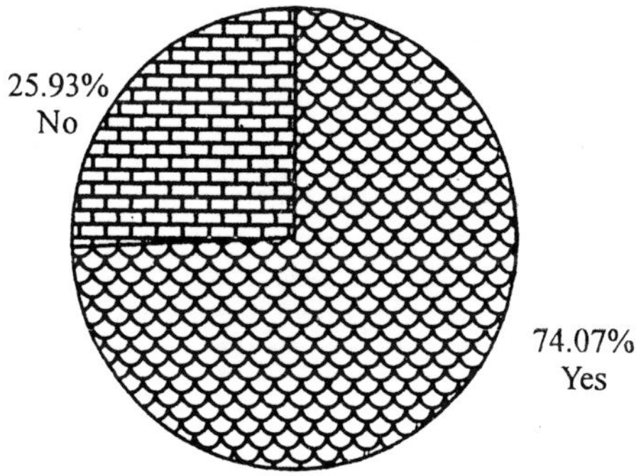

Interest in Local Culture and Cuisine

Visitors showed lot of interest in local culture including local folk

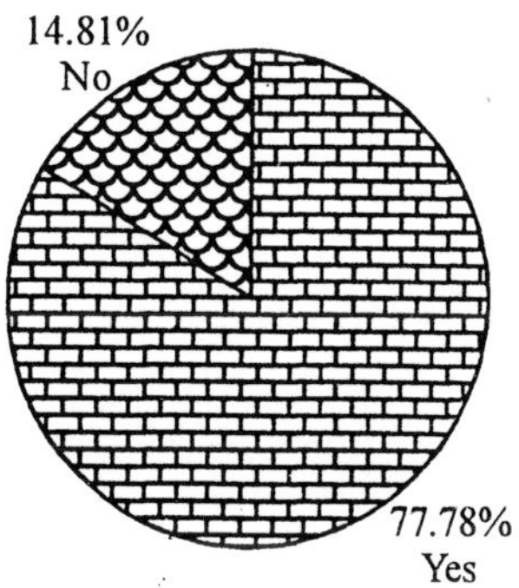

Interested in local cuisine

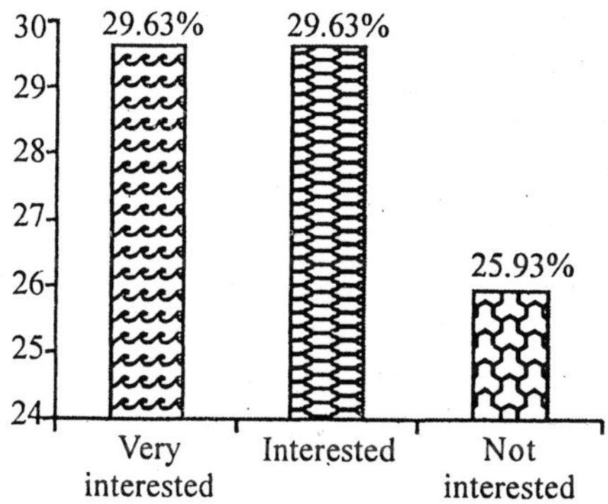

Interested in local culture

songs and dances. Visitors were also found to be interested in local cuisine.

Villagers Perception

Villagers' Profile

For the purpose of villagers' perception two adjoining villages named Mendora and Chichli were selected. These villages, being closest to the ecotourism destination area, were considered for the study.

Description	*Mendora*	*Chichli*
Number of families	64	32
Population	650	187
Total agriculture land (acres)	Nil	77A
Livestock	80	191
Distance from ecotourism	2 kms	3 kms
Destination area	The village is on way to the area	This village is situated on the other side of the area.
Village area	8 acres	5 acres
Communities	3-ST, SC, General	2-ST, SC

Traditional Business of the Area

The traditional businesses of the area are agriculture (30%), Labour (30%), animal husbandry (23.3%) and remaining people are involved in fishing (15.3%).

Traditional Business of the area	*%*
Agriculure	30.7
Labour	30.7
Animal Husbandry	23.3
Fishing	15.3

Present Occupation

Most of the villagers of these two villages are occupied in 'animal husbandry' followed by nursery (plantation), agriculture, cowdung selling, Tendu leaves collection, fishing and others.

Options	%
Animal Husbandry	72
Nursery	52
Agriculure	21
Cowdung selling	17
Tendu Leaves collection	13
Fising	11
Others	3

Handicraft and Articraft of the Area

Villagers feel that the *broom,* which is presently being made for self-consumption, can have potential as handicraft. Besides this, some ladies are also involved in *Rangoli.*

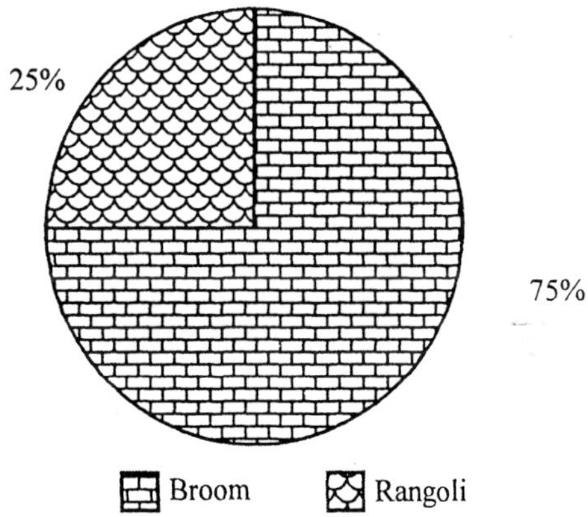

Conservation Activities by Committee

'Mendora Village Forest Committee' contributes to the conservation of forest. The committee is involved in plantation, fencing, checking illegal felling of trees, protection from fire, land filling, sanitation works etc.

Conservation Activities	%
Plantation	70.2
Fencing	15.7
Checking illegal felling of trees	8.5
Protection from fire	2.8
Land filling	1.4
Sanitation work	1.4

Awareness about Ecotourism

Most of the villagers are aware about purpose of the visit to the area by visitors, thus they are aware of ecotourism in their own perception. Nearly 76 per cent of them are aware of ecotourism and related activities.

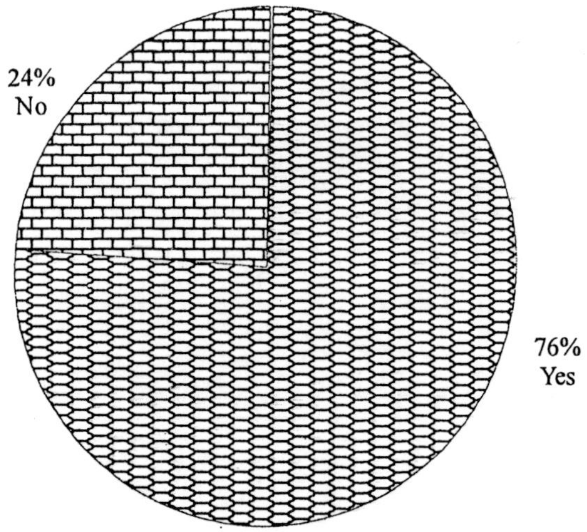

Reasons for Tourism

Through the perception of their interaction with the visitors, the villagers consider that people usually visit the place for picnic and recreation, to enjoy the nature, wildlife, fares and festivals, adventure sports and for religious purpose.

Reasons	*% response*
Picnic and recreation	60
Natural beauty	48
Wildlife seeing	13
Fire and festivals	10
Adventure sports	03
Temple	02

Types of Tourists

As per the villagers' perception about 43.4 per cent people are local people who come from in and around Bhopal, while 42.2 per cent are outsiders, who come from different places. It is interesting to note that foreign tourists (14.4%) also visit the area as guests of the local people.

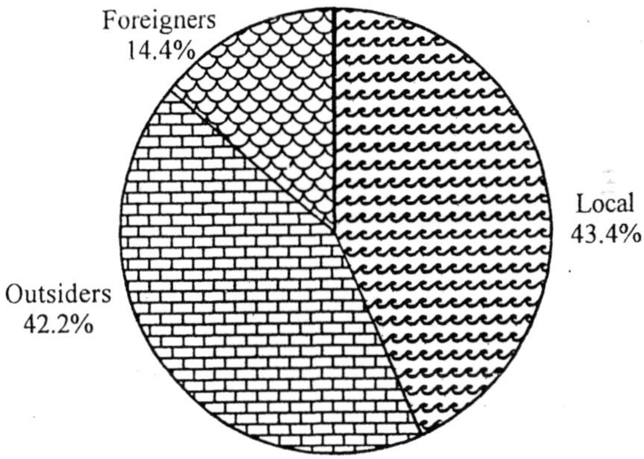

Age Class of the Tourists

According to the villagers most of the people who visit the area belong to the young generation (between 18-30 years), followed by middle class (31-50), children (below 18) and aged people (above 50).

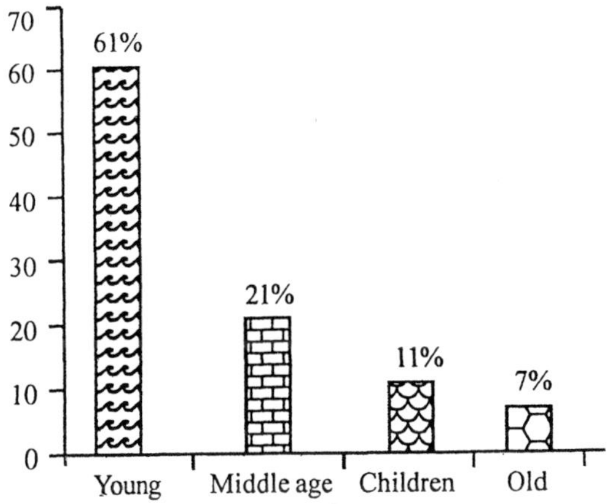

Benefits from Tourism

It has been observed that only a small percentage of local people are benefited from tourism. The main beneficiaries are petty shopkeepers, e.g., grocery store, tea stall.

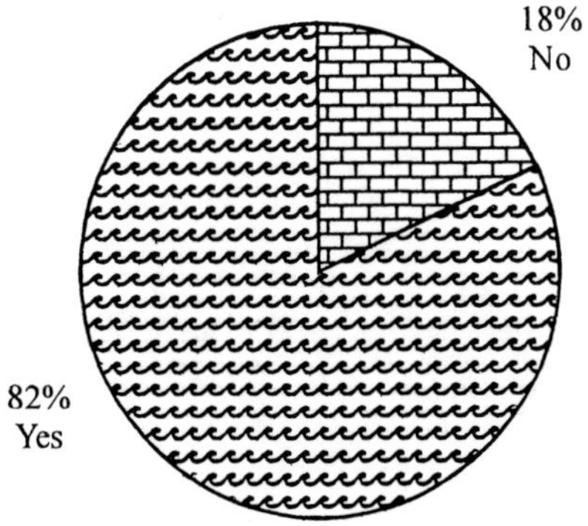

Willingness to Host Tourist

About 72 per cent people are in favour of hosting tourists, while 23 per cent are not in favour of tourism. 5 per cent people did not respond.

Willingness of Community to Control Tourism

Nearly 75 per cent of the villagers have been found to be interested

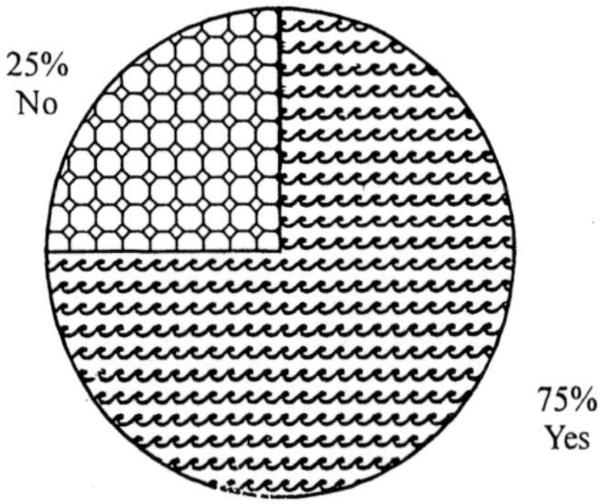

in community control of the local tourism. They are of the opinion that village level forest committees could take over the activities of the tourism.

Interested to be Associated with Ecotourism

About 75 per cent of the villagers are willing to be associated with ecotourism and related activities. They are of the opinion that this may improve their economic status as they will get more opportunities to earn through tourism. Showing interest in various enterprises and earning activities, about 23 per cent people want to establish small shops, 23 per cent want to become tourist guides, 19 per cent are in favour of establishing hotels or restaurants, followed by trading (10.7%), general employment (8%), self-employment (5%), folklore and handicraft (2.2%), cottage industry (1.1%) and adventure sports (1.1%). Significantly, as against the opinion of men, the women appeared apprehensive that their children might be affected by undesirable behaviour and lifestyle of some of the tourists.

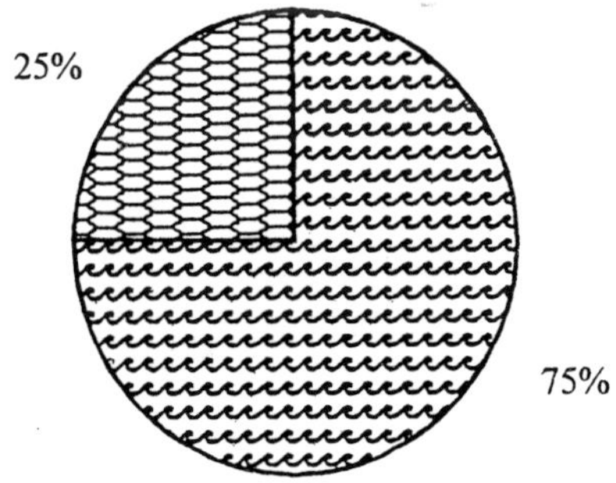

Infrastructure Need

The villagers of Mendora and Chichli villages reported that in order to adopt ecotourism for enhancing their economy, they need certain basic facilities for tourism development. About 18 per cent wanted infrastructural facility, followed by drinking water (12.5%), waste management and disposal facility (9.4%), electricity (9.4%), roads (9.4%), transportation (8.9%), communication (8.0%), Hoardings (6.7%), men and women toilets (6.7%), police station (4.9%), children park (3.1%), speed breakers (2.2%), medical facility (0.4%).

Community Based Implementation

Villagers were interested in ecotourism ventures if launched at the village level so as to enable their youths to get better job opportunities. Besides the male, women may also earn through home run centres of *papad* and pickles, tailoring and stitching, local cuisine.

Villagers Expectations

Capacity building

Villagers appeared quite clear that to take up ecotourism as an economic venture they require capacity building specially for :

- Entrepreneurship development (self-employment ventures).
- Tourism activities (guides/management).
- Small scale industries like making of *papad, achar,* basket weaving and stitching.

Financial support : The villagers also consider that some initial financial support is essential to invest in small scale industries, shops, dairy, livestock, raw materials, starting business etc.

Requirements	%
Building	17.9
Drinking water facility	12.5
Waste management facility	9.8
Electricity	9.4
Roads	9.4
Transportation	8.9
Communication facility (STD booth)	8.0
Boarding on the road	6.7
Basic Toilet facility	6.7
Police station	4.9
Children park	3.1
Speed breakers	2.2
Medical facility	0.4

Infrastructure development : Villagers feel that some infrastructures development are required for operation of the whole tourism activities specially the sheds and other logistics.

Institutionalisation and regulations : The villagers firmly believe that in order to institutionalize the process, some regulatory measures are required. Institutional mechanism is considered necessary for providing logistics, support services, fuel supply (cowdung etc.).

Reactions

Negative

- Villagers do not like tourists' behaviour to spread dirt and wastes anywhere on roads and other places thus spoiling the area by dumping empty bottles and waste food in water resulting in garbage and pungent smell.
- *"Gundagardi"* (hooliganism) is increasing because of tourism; sometimes youngsters come and shout under intoxication causing irritation to the people.
- Careless drinking/intoxication leads to dirty atmosphere.
- Few women complained that the tourists should not be allowed to enter the area as their growing up children may easily copy their bad habits.

Positive

- Some people running road side small shops of tea and snacks are benefited from tourists while others do not get much benefit.

Suggestions by Villagers

- Hoardings at prime locations should be raised for drawing the attention of visitors towards tourists' code of conduct and better civic sense.
- Efforts should be made to educate tourists about proper disposal

of waste in order to foster eco-friendly atmosphere and clean environment.

- A check-post at the entry and near the dam be established to monitor anti-social, undesirable and accidental possibilities.
- Entry fee may be imposed.
- Fishing in the dam should be allowed so that the local community may be benefited.
- Publicity campaign be launched to enlighten the tourists as well as the villagers about environmental laws, rules and regulations framed by the government from time to time.
- Banners like " Make Your Trip Green and Clean", "Wandering one gathers honey", "Enjoy Nature—the Glory of God" be put up on all over the area.

Conclusions

1. The area has tremendous potential of ecotourism and with proper organized planning and implementation, ecotourism can make a breakthrough for the conservation and economic development of the area.
2. The CBE module can be implemented as the local people are aware and sensitive about the tourism ventures, thus they can be involved in planning and implementation of the ecotourism.
3. Most villagers strongly feel that ecotourism should be encouraged and more and more ecotours be promoted. While there is liking for tourists, there is strong disliking as well for the non-environmental tourist behaviours of contributing pollution.
4. There is need for capacity building for providing them opportunities for starting business at small-scale level. The youths of the village are very much interested to be a part of ecotourism to act as tourist guides.
5. Women are also interested to take up the ecotourism related activities.

6. There is need to streamline the functioning of the village forest committee with a view to involve villagers in the development and management of the area.
7. An integrated holistic plan for the community-based ecotourism should be prepared through the involvement of all stakeholders and implemented through the local people and a strategy for the sustainable ecotourism management should also be evolved for all such areas.

REFERENCES

Cater, Erlet and Gwen Lowman (Eds), (1994). *Ecotourism : A Sustainable Option.* John Wiley and Sons, England.

Ceballos-Lascurian, Hector, (1996). *Tourism, Ecotourism and Protected Areas.* Cambridge, UK : International Union for Conservation of Nature and Natural Resources (IUCN).

Coltman, Michael M. (1989). *Tourism Marketing.* Van Nostrand Reinhold, New York.

Commonwealth Department of Tourism, (1994). *National Ecotourism Strategy,* Australian Government Service, Canberra, Australia.

Eagles, P.F.G., (1996). Issues in tourism management in Parks : The experience in Australia. *Australian Leisure,* Vol. 7, No. 2, pp. 29–37.

Figgis, P. (1993). Ecotourism: Special interest of major direction? *Habitat,* 21 (1): 8–11.

Figgis, P. (1994). *Ecotourism : Panacea, Plague or Possibility.* Eighth Richard Jones Memorial Lecture, October. University of Tasmania, Centre for Environmental Studies, Hobart.

Gunn, Clare A. (1988). *Tourism Planning.* Taylor and Francis, New York.

Harris, R. and N. Leiper (Eds) (1995). *Sustainable Tourism: An Australian Perspective.* Butterworth-Heinemann, Chatswood, NSW.

Lindberg, Kreg and Deonal, E. Hawkins (Eds) (1999). *Ecotourism: A Guide for Planners and Managers.* Vol I, North Bennington, VT, USA : The Ecotourism Society. Natraj Publishers, Dehradun, India.

Lindberg, Kreg, Meganepler Wood and David Engeldrum (Eds) (1999). *Ecotourism: A Guide for Planners and Managers.* Vol. II, North Bennington, VT, USA : The Ecotourism Society. Natraj Publishers, Dehradun, India.

Kamra, Krishnan A. (2001). *Economics of Ecotourism.* Kanishka Publishers, New Delhi.

Nelson, J.G. (1994). The spread of ecotourism: some planning implications. *Environmental Conservation, 21 (3)* : 248-255.

Sagsti, F. and M. Colby (1993). Eco-Development and Perspectives on Global Change from Developing Countries. In : *Global Accord*, Ed Chourci N., MIT Press, London

W.T.O. (1984). Economic review of world tourism. World Tourism Organisation, Madrid.

W.T.O. (1991). Yearbook of Tourism Statistics. World Tourism Organisation, Madrid.

Wight, P. (1993). Sustainable ecotourism : balancing economic, environmental and social goals within an ethical framework, *The Journal of Tourism Studies,* Vol. 4, No. 2, pp. 2–10.

W.T.O. (1993). Sustainable tourism development : Guide for local planners. A tourism and environment publication. World Tourism Organisation.

W.T.O. (1998). Guide for local authorities on developing sustainable tourism. A tourism and environment publication. World Tourism Organisation.

10

RELEVANCE OF CARRYING CAPACITY AND ECO-DEVELOPMENT LINKAGES FOR SUSTAINABLE ECOTOURISM

A.K. BHATTACHARYA AND SUCHITRA BANERJEE

Introduction

The understanding of the concept of Carrying Capacity (CC) as a determinant of Sustainable Ecotourism (SET) raises many issues which suggest further analysis of the existing concept of CC and exploring different viable models for using CC as an effective tool for SET. CC has been defined differently in different perspectives but because of the complexities of variables associated with CC it has not been possible to arrive at any simple holistic definition of CC, which could be applied and used with respect to SET. Most of the definitions of CC mainly relate to the visual impacts of the total load of the number of tourists on the physical environment along with some notional impact on social, biological and psychological environments. These impacts endure the limitations of being notional, unexplained and non-measurable. The absence of certain well defined verifiable indicators and quantitative variables of CC makes the whole phenomenon more complex and also makes it difficult to establish linkages between CC and SET.

Some of the researchers (WTO, 1984; O'Reilly, 1986; Pearce, 1989) have reservations about the usefulness of CC, as they consider that CC has very limited use in SET, whereas others (Romeril, 1989; Martin and Uysal, 1990; Hunter and Green, 1995) appreciate that CC is an essential measurement for SET and it has further been accepted as an effective tool for tourism managers by many researchers (Wall, 1983; Williams and Gill, 1994; Hunter and Green, 1995). Therefore, the premonition that CC cannot be measured quantitatively and hence has no practical value is a matter of concern and demands further research works, because the quantitative measurement of CC has not been possible mainly owing to lack of appropriate research data (Romeril, 1989; Buckley, 1995) and also adherence to the traditional approaches (Williams and Gill, 1994). Matching our requirements a system can be evolved to assign empirical values for quantitative estimation of CC. Statistical and mathematical correlationships for the quantitative measurement of CC can be developed by using Environment Impact Assessment (EIA) techniques and matrices (Tivy, 1973). Impacts can be quantified in many cases and gauged in others, which means that they may be measured and quantified in discreet ways. Empirical models for determination of quantitative measurement of CC (Canestrelli and Costa, 1991) need to be further verified and modified with more field research data and experiments.

Significantly more investigations and information are required regarding the cumulative impacts associated with ecotourism (Stabler, 1994) as the understanding of the cumulative impacts is very essential to analyse the total CC for SET. By adopting an alternative approach through identifying and establishing the appropriate factors influencing CC, it is possible to use the CC management technique for SET (Williams and Gill, 1994). In India, as in the case of most of the developing countries, ecotourism is on taking off stage and growing rapidly. On one hand, as a result of the gradual phenomenal increase in the population of human and livestock, there is constant consequential increase in biotic pressure on the natural resources including the forest lands, whereas on other, concomitantly, the ecotourism is assuming a larger dimension, which might result into a conflict in sustainability of development. Therefore, it is appropriate and high time to devise and standardise tools which might help to derive a balance between these two challenges and evolve a realistic and pragmatic package of solutions for managing these challenges. With the existing knowledge, it appears that the technique of CC can be used as a tool for meeting these long term challenges for better management of natural resources for SET.

Carrying Capacity for SET

The concept of Carring Capacity with respect to SET needs to be perceived in a different perspective and requires the visualization of the whole process with a more comprehensive viewpoint. The concept of CC is very old in wildlife management, and was used for the first time by Dasmann in 1945 (Wall, 1983) for assessing the capacity of the forests for grazing by animals. The technique of CC is very pertinent and has special relevance for the protected areas (PAs) for analyzing the interactions of the biotic pressure, ecotourism and PAs ecosystem to maintain the natural equilibrium, and the judicious and scientific determination of CC can serve to be an effective tool for the management of PAs and SET. Since the primary objective of the PAs is the management of wildlife, therefore, biodiversity conservation becomes the priority area for the CC consideration in PAs. The definition of CC as propounded and applied by Lindsay (1980) for PAs emphasises all aspects concerning SET but apparently does not take into consideration the probable long term impacts of ecotourism on biodiversity. The qualitative and quantitative implications of ecotourism on wildlife, viz. species diversification, health, and even breeding need to be essentially considered for the determination of CC for SET in PAs. Thus the quantitative measurement of CC for certain variables also becomes a prerequisite for assessing the scope for SET in PAs. The example of occasional discontinuation of the visit of the migratory Siberian cranes indicates that sometimes the attitude and behaviour of the ecotourists plays a significant role as a variable of CC towards SET in PAs. In India and other developing countries the displacement of the communities from the National Parks (NPs) and their rehabilitation may act as a limiting factor for CC towards SET. Thus the concept of destination area as extended by Hovinen

(1982) and Martin and Uysal (1990) needs to be redefined or modified for the Indian NPs, specially when the communities have been displaced outside the NPs areas. Because of the ban on prevailing community rights in NPs and Wildlife Sanctuaries (WLSs), the impact of ecotourism in such cases goes beyond the destination areas through the ecotourists and NPs based community linkages. Thus in order to determine CC for SET in PAs it becomes essential to include the impact of ecotourism even outside the destination area, taking into consideration the interrelationship of NPs based community and ecotourists visualising both human and non-human factors. In reference to SET in PAs the level of tolerance of the ecosystem is more important variable *vis-a-vis* the load of number of ecotourists. Unscientific management of ecotourism in PAs may cause more environmental damage than that caused to any other destination areas (Ashton, 1992). For PAs the ecotourism may be designated as 'Environmental Tourism', which not only covers all the parameters of ecotourism but also provides a wider horizon to include all environmental factors of the destination area—both micro and macro—viz. ecological, social, cultural, psychological, anthropological etc.

Eco-Development (ED)

The ED model, originally advanced by UNEP (Dasmann, 1985), aims towards an ecologically sustainable form of development through the economic sustainable development of local communities dependent on the environment for their basic needs. Thus ED attempts at overall development through which the local communities become self-reliant to achieve both their basic needs and help them in sustaining biodiversity. Some researchers prefer to use the concept of ED for both ecological and economic development, and thus consider that 'eco' stands for both 'ecological' and 'economic' (Gupta, 1988). The concept of ED has been pursued through a series of projects in management practice of PAs (Collins, 1994; Rao and Geisler, 1990). IUCN (1984) has reported human encroachment as the second of the top ten kinds of threat facing

43 of world's most threatened PAs, which manifests the significance of ED in the management of the PAs.

The term 'ED' has been adopted in India since 1980s and a number of definitions have been proposed (World Bank, 1995). Most commonly it has been applied in connection with PAs such as NPs and WLSs to define a strategy for protecting ecologically valuable areas from unsustainable or otherwise unacceptable pressures resulting from the needs and activities of the people living in and around such areas. It is based on the assumption that if alternative natural and social resources are created in areas peripheral to the PAs, exploitation of resources within the PAs will be reduced. There is also an assumption that the involvement of the PAs management in the creation of employment opportunities in fringe areas resources, which may include fodder, veterinary services, water services, and other village infrastructures, will motivate communities to collaborate in the protection of forest areas. ED involves participatory management of resources but communities do not receive direct benefits of forest produce from the PAs. In other forest areas managed through Joint Forest Management, the communities dependent on them derive usufruct benefits by sharing of products. This anomaly in usufruct sharing mechanism in PAs and adjoining non-PAs may lead to a conflict in sustainability of PAs and this issue needs to be examined from the viewpoint of management.

In many of Indian States including Madhya Pradesh, Gujarat, West Bengal and others, the term ED has been used in a more general way to denote ED of villages close to forest lands. The more general usage is referred to as 'Village Resource Development Programme', which is similar to ED in trying to reduce pressure on forest land by providing alternative sources of income. The proposed strategy for biodiversity conservation would be to focus on improved PAs management of high priority areas of biological importance, in which human impacts are readily manageable. Also the management of lower priority would be maintained through fewer resources. PAs management would be complemented by ED in areas peripheral to PAs. The PAs network, in particular, linkages between existing PAs, would be developed through identification of relatively undisturbed satellite areas and for the intervening zone, the preparation of management plans that are compatible with biodiversity conservation. Thus the issues related to ED with respect to new strategy of management of PAs and its impact on SET need to be thoroughly examined.

Carrying Capacity and Eco-Development Linkages for Set

The preceding paras clearly suggest that in the management of PAs the ED approach is going to have great impact on CC with respect to SET. The impact of communities living in and around the PAs on the CC of the destination area needs to be critically examined for the determination of total CC. The different indices of interrelationship and interactions between the PAs and the dependent communities have to be linked with other factors/ variables of CC. Whether the local communities along with the ecotourists can be used as contrivance for conservation of biodiversity and whether ecotourism can be practised as an incentive for the local people for the conservation leading to SET are challenging issues to be addressed by the managers of PAs, and the success of SET in PAs will largely depend on this complex but natural relationship. The knowledge of CC-ED linkages should prove to be an effective tool for evolving suitable strategy for both integrated management of PAs and also environmentally compatible ecotourism. Participation of local people in managing PAs becomes essential for a fundamental shift away from the old conventional approach to conservation (Williams and Gill, 1994). The necessity for incorporating the needs and perceptions of local people in the establishment and management of the resources was first emphasized by Man and Biosphere Programme in 1979 (UNESCO, 2002).

Conservation of biodiversity and integration of protected area management with the needs of local people and their development has emerged as a priority for the management and sustainability of NPs and SET (Wells and Brandon, 1995; Buckley, 1995).

Conservation, thus, requires a perspective which stretches beyond the NPs boundaries. Many case studies have indicated that the community involvement in the SET of PAs has not been very effective mainly because of two reasons. First, the participation has not been beneficiary oriented and, therefore, has not been sustainable and secondly, methods of participation have not been matched with requirements and thinking of the local people. Although community involvement has widely been accepted as an essential key element and prerequisite for PAs management and SET (Sadler, 1990; Burchett, 1991; Wight, 1993; Lay, 1996), but no pragmatic and effective devices for active involvement have so far been evolved. Thus it becomes imperative that specific models for community involvement are required to be evolved for better cooperative relationship between PAs and local people (Wells and Brandon, 1995). Long term success of SET ultimately depends upon community perception and involvement in planning and management of SET (Craik, 1991).

World Bank and Future Strategy for SET

In countries, where World Bank sponsored forestry projects are being implemented, the SET will largely depend upon the strategy being adopted for PAs management under the project. In India the World Bank Forestry Project encompasses the component of Biodiversity Conservation for PAs, which aims at improved management of high priority PAs through provisions of support for development of management plans, staff training, equipments, and other facilities. There is special provision for funds to support the development of alternative resources of income for communities resident within PAs and in areas peripheral to them. A low level of project funding would be made available for low priority PAs whilst the identification and planning of linkages to complete the PAs network would be finalized. It would be interesting to examine the impact of the provisions of the project on the management of the PAs with respect to the SET.

Scope for Research

Based on the analysis of the existing knowledge of the subject, as discussed in the preceding paragraphs above, and the evaluation of the strength and gaps in the knowledge, the following issues need to be taken into consideration :

1. With the growing environmental awareness, the ecotourism is going to assume very large dimension in the recent future, more widely in the developing countries, and the PAs will be the main destination areas for the majority of ecotourism.
2. CC can serve as one of the most effective tools for the management of PAs with respect to promotion of SET. The lack of adequate field data and research work act as an impediment to the use of CC as a practical management supplement for SET. Relevant techniques are required to be generated to analyse the cumulative impacts affecting the total CC.
3. It is possible to evolve certain correlationship/matrices for the quantitative measurement of CC for SET in PAs. With the help of some relevant research work and field data practical models for quantitative measurement of CC may be developed.
4. Because of lack of certain well defined objectively verifiable indicators the effectiveness of CC technique for SET in PAs has been impaired. Based on practical research and field data some simple responsive applicable indicators may be formalized for the use and monitoring of CC techniques for SET in PAs.
5. The process of ED influences CC largely in PAs, and the CC in PAs is regulated by the factors involved in the ecologically oriented economic development of the communities dependent on the PAs. The analyses of the synergistic impact of the ecotourism and the communities on the PAs by scrutinising the CC-ED linkages may provide some pragmatic solutions for the challenges likely to be met for SET in PAs.

6. Involvement of communities living in and around PAs is an essential element for SET. Realistic and pragmatic models ensuring active involvement of communities may be evolved by examining and extending CC-ED linkages for SET. This will in turn facilitate SET and also protect PAs which will contribute to both management of PAs and SET.
7. Under the new forestry projects being assisted by World Bank there is a distinct shift in strategy of management of PAs, from the traditional top bottom approach to bottom top approach, the emphasis being on community participation in forest management. The implementation will have many challenges mainly because the existing models of people's participation have not been found to be effective.
8. In spite of the obvious significance and relevance of CC for SET, no organised study on the CC with respect to SET in PAs in India has so far been pursued. A detailed pilot study should be fruitful to develop a sound strategy for SET in many developing countries.

Parameters of Further Investigations

In the light of the above mentioned background it clearly emerges that some more intensive and integrated research works are necessary to:

(a) redefine the CC for PAs, with respect to SET, specially in developing countries,

(b) evolve certain applicable models for quantitative measurement of CC,

(c) determine ED and CC linkages for SET, and

(d) design appropriate management modules suitable for SET in PAs.

In order to bridge the gaps in the existing knowledge on the subject the research should aim at the following objectives:

1. To critically analyse the process and frameworks of CC in PAs with respect to SET, by identifying the various factors/

parameters linked with and/or influencing CC and their interactions and cumulative impacts.

2. To develop certain empirical/statistical correlationships/ matrices for the determination of quantitative measurement of CC with respect to SET in PAs.
3. To study the linkages between the CC and ED in PAs by evaluating the qualitative and quantitative impacts of the communities on the CC—both individual and synergistic.
4. To identify and standardize certain objectively verifiable and applicable indicators for CC and ED linkages and SET based on the field standards.
5. To evolve certain realistic models/package for CC and ED linkages for the management of PAs and SET.
6. To critically evaluate the cumulative and synergistic impacts of the World Bank Forestry Project on the management of the PAs and SET.
7. To develop an appropriate package for training and education for SET for all levels involved in ecotourism including the local communities.

Design and Methodology for Research

The methodology of the study should, however, be decided on the basis of the available literature and preliminary reconnaissance survey of the area, and nevertheless, and following criteria may be taken into consideration while finalising the methodology:

1. Review of the available literature/case studies and collection of data available on the subject.
2. Critical examination and analysis of the existing management practices and Working/Management Plans being implemented and their impacts in PAs with respect to SET and scrutiny of the mechanisms of various operations.
3. Use of participatory rural appraisal/rapid rural appraisal techniques for the study of the correlationships of communities and PAs with respect to their dependence on PAs and their involvement in management practices.

4. Development of empirical correlationships for quantitative measurement of CC on the basis the existing EIA techniques.
5. The study area (PAs) may be selected on the basis of following norms :
   - 5.1. The National Park attracting the maximum number of ecotourists.
   - 5.2. The National Park receiving the minimum number of ecotourists.
   - 5.3. The largest National Park (in terms of area).
   - 5.4. The smallest National Park.
   - 5.5. The National Park where ED and community participation are successful.
   - 5.6. The National Park where ED and community participation are reportedly failure.
   - 5.7. Comparison of the observations with those of NPs of some other developing countries and also with those of developed countries, where ecotourism is rapidly growing as an industry.

Conclusion

There is considerable scope for research on the concept of CC and its use as a management tool for ecotourism in PAs, specially in developing countries, where the ecotourism may add to the cumulative impact of the already existing biotic pressure on the PAs. Exploratory research is essential to evolve some viable mechanisms and models to involve the local communities in the management of ecotourism in these areas. Sustainability of ecotourism will largely depend on the active involvement of the local communities. Ecotourism and ED linkages may probably be used as tool for the conservation of the natural resources and sustainable development.

Summary

The concept and significance of carrying capacity with respect to

SET has been explained and analysed in the chapter. The emerging importance of CC and ED linkages in ecotourism and wildlife management has been addressed and critically examined. The scope of further research, methodology and bibliography for further readings in the field have been suggested.

REFERENCES

Ashton, R. (1992). World Tourism trends in Tourism and Conservation (Ecotourism). In : *Proceedings of the 1992 World Congress on Adventure Travel and Ecotourism.* The Adventure Travel Society Inc., Engel Wood, Columbia. pp. 67-73.

Buckley, R.C. (1995). Where Tourism and Ecology Meet. International Conference: *Eco-Tourism: Concept, Design and Strategy*, February 6-8, Bangkok, Institute of Eco-Tourism, Srinakharinwirot University.

Burchett, C. (1991). Ecologically sustainable development and its relationship to Aboriginal tourism in the Northern Territory. *Ecotourism: Incorporating the Global Classroom*, Canberra, Bureau of Tourism Research.

Canestrelli, E. and Costa, P. (1991). Tourist CC—A Fuzzy Approach. *Annals of Tourism Research*, 18 : 295-311.

Collins, C. (1994). Conservationists call on tourism industry to join green movement. The Australian, 14 April, p. 6.

Craik, J. (1991). *Resorting to Tourism*: Cultural Policies for Tourist Development in Australia. Allen and Unwin, North Sydney.

Dasmann, R.F. (1985). Achieving the sustainable use of species and ecosystems. *Landscape Plan*, 12 (3) : 211-219.

Gupta, A. (1988). *Ecology and Development in the Third World*. Routledge, U.S.A.

Hovinen, G.R. (1982). Visitors Cycle : Outlook for Tourism in Lancaster Country. *Annals of Tourism Research*, 9 : 565-583.

Hunter, C. and Green, H. (1995). *Tourism and the Environment : A Sustainable Relationship*. Routledge, London.

IUCN (1994). *Ecotourism Consultancy Programme*. IUCN, Mexico.

Lay, B. (1996). Community Involvement in the Establishment of an Access Network to Scenic Areas. Paper presented at the Best Practice Ecotourism Conference, Coolangatta, Qld.

Lindsay, J. (1980). Compatibility planning for different types of outdoor recreation and resources. In : *Tourism Planning and Development Issues* (D. Hawkins *et al.*, eds) pp. 138-47, Washington DC, George Washington University.

Martin, B.S. and Uysal, M. (1990). An examination of the relationship between carrying capacity and tourism lifecycle : management and policy implications. *Jour Env Manag*, 31 : 327-333.

O'Reilly, A.M. (1986). Tourism carrying capacity. *Tourism Management*, 7 (4), 254–258

Pearce, Douglas (1989). Tourist Development. II ed. Longman Scientific.

Rao, K. and Geisler, C. (1990). The social consequences of protected areas development for resident populations. Society and Natural Resources. 3:19-32. (www.gu.edu.au/centre/capsm/Corbett.htm-101k -)

Romeril, M. (1989). Tourism and the environment-accord or discord? *Tourism Management*, 10 (3) : 204-208.

Sadler, B. (1990). Sustainable development, northern realities and the design and implementation of regional conservation strategies. In : *Achieving sustainable development through northern conservation strategies*, pp. 3-31, University of Calgary Press, Calgary.

Stabler, M. (1994). An economic critique of tourism environmental auditing. *Tourism Research and Education in Australia: Proceedings from the Tourism Research and Education Conferences*, Eds Faulkner, B., Fagence, M., Davidson, M. and Craig Smith S. Bureau of Tourism Research, Canberra.

Tivy, Joy (1973). *The Concept of Determination of CC of Recreational Land in the USA*. Countryside Communication, Perth, Scotland. Occasional Paper No. 3, Perth, Scotland.

UNESCO (2002). UNESCO, Man and the Biosphere Programme (WWW.UNESCO.ORG/MAB/, 3 AUG, 2002)

Wall, G. (1983). Cycles and Capacity : A Contradiction in Terms ! *Annals of Tourism Research*, 268-269.

Wells, M. and Brandon, K. (1995). People and Park : Linking protected area management with local communities. The World Bank, World Wildlife Fund, USAID, Washington DC.

Wight, P.A. (1993). Ecotourism : Ethics or Eco-Sell? *Journal of Travel Research*, 31 (3) : 3-9.

Williams, P.W. and Gill, A. (1994). Tourism CC management issues. In : *Global Tourism : The next decade*, Ed Theobold W. Butterworth Heinemann, Oxford.

World Bank (1995). The India Eco-development Project : Project Document. The World Bank-GEF, World Bank, World Bank India.

WTO (1984). Economic Review of World Tourism. World Tourism Organisation, Madrid.

11

ECOTOURISM IN MADHYA PRADESH

SUCHITRA BANERJEE, YOGESH DUBEY AND A.K. BHATTACHARYA

Madhya Pradesh lies in the heart of India covering an area of 3,08,000 sq km making it one of the largest States in India bordering seven other states—Uttar Pradesh, Jharkhand, Orissa, Andhra Pradesh, Maharashtra, Gujarat and Rajasthan.

Madhya Pradesh consists largely of a plateau streaked with hill ranges of Vindhyas and Satpuras. The hills give rise to main river systems—the Narmada and the Tapti flowing from east to west and Chambal, Sone, Betwa, Mahanadi and Indravati from west to east. Intersected by these meandering rivers and dotted with hills and lakes the State is endowed with rich natural setting and variety of landscapes and biodiversity.

Although the modern State of Madhya Pradesh came into being in 1956, its cultural heritage is ancient. The State is also extremely rich in its biological resources. Almost one-third of the State is forested and offers unique and exciting panorama of wildlife. Madhya Pradesh also known, as Tiger State is the only State which harbours the largest population of Tiger, the most endangered species of large cats in India.

Most of the Ecotourism, under whatsoever name has been practised in Madhya Pradesh has invariably been in the Protected Areas. However due to utter lack of infrastructure, trained manpower and absence of separate contingent staff for visitors use and interpretations are other serious impediments in the way of development of Ecotourism. Even at the established sites tourists often return without exploring and enriching themselves through a variety of experience due to lack of facilities.

Protected Areas, owing to severe pressure and interference stemming from dependence of local people on various resources for their sustenance and livelihood couple with severe grazing and lopping pressure created by large number of cattle from within and outside the area, tourism becomes a low priority item on the overall agenda of the Protected Area management.

Sharing of benefits with the local people is another issue. Even at highly visited sites the benefits of tourism has not percolated to the host communities, which continue to live in a state of abject impoverishment (Khajurao being a glaring example). This may be because the direct stakes of community living in those areas may not have been taken into consideration while formulating policies and plans. Therefore while promoting the existing tourist sites and potential new sites as Ecotourism areas, policies should be formulated such that the twin objectives of biodiversity conservation and community development are taken care of.

Existing Policy

As far as Ecotourism is concerned, there is no exclusive policy designed to see the interest of this emerging sector both at National and State levels. In all those States where Ecotourism is being practised to some extent, the compliance if at all there is by various stakeholders are only of the tourism policy and other related policies such as those of Wildlife Protection Act, 1972, Forest Conservation Act, 1980 etc. What is urgently required if this sector has to bloom is its own policies have to be formulated which would take into consideration all the necessary nitty-gritty of this sector.

In Madhya Pradesh, the only efforts towards making Eco-tourism has been the "Eco and adventure tourism policy" formulated by Tourism Department of M.P. The publications are more of a set of tourism guidelines than policies in actual terms. There is no legal mechanism to ensure protection of local culture and communities against the ill effects of improperly managed and ill planned tourism. Proponents of Ecotourism will have to be extra cautious about this possibility also.

Need for Co-ordination of Activities

It would be impossible to get desired results and meet the broad objectives without establishing linkages between different stakeholders, viz. Hoteliers, tour operators, Tourism Department, Forest department and local people. Therefore, there is a need to galvanize the collective potential of all the stakeholders and using their experience gathered over decades in fields related to Eco-tourism to move forward towards effective implementation of environmental norms in this new regime for better environmental protection and sustainable development.

Identification of Tourism Sites

All the tourism sites which will cater to the interests of different tourism groups will be identified in phases and developed. Some of the identified tourism sites have been mentioned in Table 11.1.

Table 11.1 : Major Tourist Sites

	Destination	*Tourist interest*
1.	Bandhavgarh NP	Nature, Historical
2.	Kanha NP	Nature
3.	Madhav NP (Shivpuri)	Historical, Nature
4.	Gwalior	Historical
5.	Pachmarhi	Nature, Historical
6.	Sanchi	Religious, Historical
7.	Amarkantak	Religious
8.	Chitrakoot	Religious
9.	Maheshwar	Religious
10.	Omkareshwar	Religious
11.	Orchha	Historical, Religious
12.	Ujjain	Religious
13.	Mandu	Historical
14.	Bodhghat	Religious

Ecotourism Sites

Similarly the ecotourism sites of the States will be identified and developed as per the ecotourism objectives based on site specific ecotourism plans. Some of the identified ecotourism sites have been mentioned in Table 11.2.

Table 11.2 : Potential Ecotourism Sites

	Destination	*Tourism interest*
1.	Ratapani WLS* (Obedullaganj)	Nature, Historical
2.	Kanger Valley NP** (Bastar)	Nature, Historical, Religious
3.	Panna NP and adjoining forests (Panna)	Nature, Historical, Religious, Adventure
4.	Pench WLS and Sakata-Rukhad forests (Seoni)	Nature
5.	Noradehi WLS (Sagar)	Nature
6.	Rani Durgawati WLS (Daboh)	Nature, Historical
7.	Satpura NP and Bori WLS (Hoshangabad)	Nature, Religious
8.	Sanjay NP (Sidhi)	Nature
9.	Betul Forests (Betul)	Nature
10.	Tamor Pingla WLS adjoining forests (Sarguja)	Nature
11.	Buffer Zone forests of Kanha Tiger Reserve (Mandla)	Nature
12.	Barnawapara WLS (Raipur)	Nature
13.	Ralamandal WLS (Indore)	Nature
14.	Kheoni WLS (Dewas)	Nature

* WLS—Wildlife Sanctuary

** NP—National Park

Tourism Circuits

Tourism circuits and packages will be developed integrating the different types of tourism site e.g. integrating heritage of Khajuraho with wildlife tourism of Banhavgarh National Park. Some of the identified tourism circuits have been mentioned in Table 11.3.

Table 11.3 : Tourism Circuits – Packages

The Bhopal Zone :

Bhopal
Sanchi
Bhim Betka

Bhojpur
Bhopal Lakes
Ratapani WLS—Van Vihar

The Jabalpur Zone :

Amarkantak
Fossil NP
Bandhavgarh NP
Rani Durgavati WLS
Bedhaghat Marble Rocks
Kanha NP (Ecotourism)
Kanha Buffer (Ecotourism)

The Panna – Khajuraho Zone :

Panna NP
Panna Forests (Ecotourism)
Chitrakoot falls
Orchha
Shivpuri Madhav NP
Gwalior
Khajuraho
Ken-Ghariyal WLS

The Pachmarhi-Pench Zone :

Pench WLS
Rukhad-Sakata Forests (Ecotourism)
Patalkot (Chindwara) (Ecotourism)
Tamia (Chindwara)
Satpura NP
Pachmarhi
Bori WLS (Ecotourism)

The Indore Zone :

Maheshwar
Ujjain
Mandu
Ralamandal WLS (Ecotourism)
Kheoni WLS (Ecotourism)

Ecotourism facilities

In order to promote ecotourism for different target groups particular types of facilities will be required to develop under the broad framework of ecotourism. Some of the identified facilities have been mentioned in Table 11.4.

Table 11.4

Ecotourism Attractive Facilities
Eco centres
Nature trail
Interpretation inputs
Orientation centre
Visitor centre
Museum
Amphitheatre
Roadside Markets
Literature
Light and sound display
Vehicular excursions
Picnic spots
Canoeing/boating
Elephant rides
Angling
Pony rides
Village visit
Ethnic/folk dance
Bird club
Souvenir shops
Cycle trail

Operation guidelines

Specific operation guidelines for different stakeholders are required to be developed for effective ecotourism planning and implementation. A proposed set of guidelines is attached as Table 11.5.

Table 11.5 : Operations Guidelines for the Government

Delineate fringe areas around PAs and forest areas for Ecotourism.

The Ecotourism plan should be prepared by a specially constituted "planning team" with representatives from the Tourism Department, PA management, Panchayat, EDC/FPC/VFC.

The planning should be flexible, site—specific and participatory and should form part of a larger Eco-regional plan for the area.

Assessment of existing infrastructure, surface transportation, air service, road, electricity, water supply, law and order situation.

The Eco-tourism package should invariably include :

Simple, adequate boarding and lodging facilities, in tune with the environment and the general setting of the landscape.

Road network within the identified tourism zone

Self-guided Nature trails

Interceptive Centres

Wayside exhibits

Signages

Observation towers

Public conveniences

Garbage disposal facility

Living quarters for staff/personnel

Structures with an exotic look causing visual pollution and non-compatible and unaesthetic architecture should be avoided.

Site-specific micro-planning for community based ecotourism should be resorted to

Providing soft loans from the "Vikas Nidhis" to identified beneficiaries.

Temporary housing structures blending with the surrounding should be encouraged.

Establishing building codes in consultation with the Panchayats (village level institution) apart from other regulations to ensure pollution free environment, with the concurrence of the respective "Zila Sarkar" (District Government).

Environmental, physical and social carrying capacities to limit the various developmental activities in the fringe area to be identified for ecotourism.

Devise mechanism to ensure continuous monitoring of adverse effects of tourism for quick redressal.

Recognize ecotourism operators, provide incentives to deserving cases and award quality labels.

Provide visitor information and interpretation services (bilingual) covering :

- "Dos" and "Don'ts"
- What to see?
- Where to see?

(Brochures, leaflets, guide service, visitor centres)

Periodic training programmes on Ecotourism should be conducted for tourism administration, planners, operators and general public.

Ensuring training Programme to the host community in :

Lodge ownership/management

Basic education and awareness

Health development for preparation

Skill development for preparation of local souvenirs as appropriate

Codes of conduct

Forest and wildlife conservation

Litter control

Forging partnerships with tourists and tourism industry

Environmental management

Evolve and implement Ecotourism package in few selected sites initially as pilot projects.

For Tour Operators/Developers:

Abide by the planning restrictions, codes and standards prescribed by the authorities.

Implementation of desired environmental principles through regulation.

Conducting EIA/environmental audits for new/ongoing Ecotourism projects.

Being sensitive to the conservation of endangered species and corridor value of the area.

Ensure construction of structures blending with the environment as per the prescribed building code.

Take into consideration the carrying capacity and sociological use-limits of the site while creating tourist facilities, and ensuring safety and conveniences of tourists.

Use local material and design as far as possible, while avoiding over construction.

The planning, architectural design and construction of tourist facilities should use Eco-friendly techniques, viz., solar energy, recycling of garbage, harvesting of rain water, natural cross-ventilation instead of AC, self-sufficiency in food through kitchen garden and farming.

Energy and water saving devices should be used apart from controlled sewage disposal.

Control of noise pollution, chemical pollution and air emissions.

Use of signages/boards as per the standard prescriptions in the code.

Reduced use of environmentally unfriendly items like asbestos, CIS, pesticides, inflammable material.

Respecting the historic and religious sites in the area.

Providing appropriate interpretive service to visitors for communication with nature and local culture.

Ensuring proper marketing of ecotourism products.

Ensuring training of staff on environmental issues.

Ensuring safety and security of visitors

Respecting local inhabitants, culture and involving them in various activities and vocations as far as possible.

For the Visitors :

Abiding by the code of conducts, "Dos" and Don'ts"

Helping conservation, apart from protecting any site natural or cultural, which may be adversely affected by tourism.

Avoiding wastage of resources.
Avoiding littering and carrying back all non-degradable litters.
Leaving the camp sites clean before departing.
Avoiding removal of plants, seeds drift-wood from the site.
Respecting local culture/customs.
Respecting holy places.
Strictly adhering to the safety precautions.

For Host Community

Respect the value of environment, cultural heritage.
Avoid overusing the area
Cooperate with the authorities in ensuring healthy Ecotourism.
Realize and react to the threat of investors who see opportunities and exploit the locals.
Be friendly with the visitors as effective "nature guides" and "conservationists".

Note : The informations are based on the unpublished communications by H S Pabla, Chief Conservator of Forests, and Suhash Kumar, Conservator of Forests, Madhya Pradesh.

12

ECOTOURISM POTENTIAL IN MADHYA PRADESH

A.K. BHATTACHARYA, YOGESH DUBEY AND ALARK SAXENA

There has been a significant growth in nature tourism all over the world. The world tourism has attained new records with half a billion-tourist arrival all over the world in spite of the recession in the previous years. Madhya Pradesh (M.P.) with its vast resources in the form of natural landscape, bio-diversity, heritage sites and adventure sites has got tremendous potential in terms of promoting Ecotourism.

Most of the Ecotourism under whatsoever name has been practised in MP has invariably been practised in the Protected Area. Madhya Pradesh has recently announced State Biodiversity Strategy and Action Plan 2002, which underlines the need of eco-development in the State to conserve its Biodiversity heritage. The Government of Madhya Pradesh had also announced its new Eco and Adventure Tourism Policy (2001-2002). These policy initiatives provide a consistent framework to explore possibilities in the Ecotourism sector. Ecotourism has become very important for the areas having rich cultural and biological heritage. This study was conducted to evaluate the Ecotourism Potential of the existing sites and also to find out new sites with Ecotourism Potential.

Out of the five identified circuits, i.e. Panna, Bhopal, Indore, Jabalpur and Pachmarhi the first three were chosen as they were found to be representative of the area. A total of 31 sites (existing and newly identified) were assessed for Ecotourism Potential. A survey was conducted to find out the tourist preferences, their problems and their requirements. The study revealed that there is a difference in the preferences of the domestic tourist as compared to the foreign tourist. The domestic tourists have an inclination towards religious tourism, while the Foreign Tourist prefer Cultural Tourism.

Most of the sites that were evaluated had good Ecotourism potential like Panna National Park, Bhopal, Mandu which had a blend of Both Cultural and Natural Resources and also had opportunities to develop a good interpretation and educational programmes which become an integral part of Ecotourism. Only a few had lower potential due to their susceptibility to impacts and lack of proper infrastructure, e.g. Maihar which is subjected to high pressure from the religious tourism. It was also found that Adventure aspect of Ecotourism is completely lacking in the State baring a few sites like Bhopal. It was also found that there is a need to increase coordination between the Forest Department and the Tourism Department for enhancing Ecotourism activities such that the forest department manages all the natural resources and the tourism department does all the marketing associated to it. There was also a need felt for greater coordination between the Forest Department and thc Adventure clubs such that Forest Department provides access to various natural resources and the Adventure club provides the tourist inflow to promote Ecotourism.

The new sites that have Ecotourism potential and the various ecotourism activities that could be started in the already existing sites are given below for two major circuits.

1.1 Panna Circuit

Maihar

Maihar is a small town 40 km South of Satna. It is already known for its religious importance as it has the famous Sharda Maa Temple. It is believed that the great legendary figures Alha and Udal still come to the temple to worship the Goddess. At present there are no ecotourism activities going around in the place. Maihar has got some lakes around it, which can be used, for activities like boating. Also there could be an Alha trek made on the same route on which the legendary figures supposedly come every morning. An education programme with the help of slide shows, posters etc. can also be developed which would make people aware of the degradation of Sharda hill due to the growing tourist pressure.

Chitrakoot (Botanical Excursion)

Chitrakoot is also famous for its religious importance. It is at a distance of 80 km North East of Satna. Chitrakoot is at the borders of Madhya Pradesh and Uttar Pradesh. Both the domestic and the foreign tourists visit the place for religious and cultural tourism respectively. It is known that the forests around Chitrakoot are very rich in medicinal herbs that are used in Ayurveda. It is unique in the sense that it has herbs of all the ten root types (*das mool*), which is rare. This uniqueness of Chitrakoot can be harnessed for its educational value and a Botanical Excursion could be planned for tourists that are interested in it. Trained and learned officers could be appointed in Chitrakoot who can take people on a Botanical Excursion and make them identify the various kinds of herbs present in the wild. Also Chitrakoot has Arogyadham, which treats people with the help of Naturopathy and Ayurveda. There is a growing demand for Ayurveda and Naturopathy. Thus this aspect of Chitrakoot could be linked with the excursion and marketed well on the lines of Kerala Tourism by the Tourism Department. There could be centres opened for tourists to come and enjoy the healing power of Naturopathy and Ayurveda and thus diversify the tourism activities.

Ken River (Kayaking / Boating)

Ken river is one of the unpolluted rivers in India. The main reason is that it does not pass through any city or town. Ken river forms the lifeline of Panna National Park. Kayaking or Boating activities can be promoted in the Ken river as the velocity of the river is not very high and there are long stretches of river without any hurdles like protruding rocks or whirlpools etc. Care should be taken here that the kayaking and boating activities do not disturb the habitat of the gharials in the river. Local people can also be involved and their capacities can be developed which could thus help us in promoting ecotourism activities in the area.

Rane Falls (Rock Climbing)

Rane Falls are falls situated on the river Ken. Rane Falls are only 17 km from Khajuraho and come in the Ken Gharial Wildlife Sanctuary. The fall has protruding rock faces that become challenging for rock climbers. There are variety of rock faces that provide opportunity to climb both for young and for experienced. The sites could be promoted by inviting various Adventure Clubs, which are involved in such activities. Since the Adventure Club would get an access to a good site and the Forest Department will get tourist, hence both the players would get benefited. Also the Tourist would be able to get a new experience. These could be promoted under supervision of trained manpower.

Bhopal Circuit

Ginnor Garh

Ginnor Garh is a fort in the Ratapani WLS. It is about 55 km from Bhopal and is situated about 6 km. inside the forest. The fort has been built by the Gond King and has got great architectural relevance as it has 6 stories and is a complete establishment with its wells and water reservoirs and huge gates. At present it is lying in ruins and there is nobody to take care of the area. The location of the fort is on the top of the highest peak of the Ratapani area. The fort is surrounded by beautiful landscape all around and looks beautiful during the rainy season.

Bhimbetka (trekking)

Bhimbetka lies 50 km South of Bhopal near to Obedullahgunj. It is known for its primitive rock paintings. There are around 600 rock shelters in and around the area spread over an area of 400 hectares. The area has got good forest. Also an important observation here is that Ginnor Fort and Bhimbetka are linked with continuous dense forest. This is a good combination and a trek could be proposed from Bhimbetka to Ginnor Garh fort where the tourist can come and enjoy the trek which moves through forest, allows the trekkers to see all the caves that are spread around and then move to Ginnor Garh fort, which will give a unique experience of a historical architecture. Local staff/people could be used to guide the tourist and reach the fort safely.

Salkanpur

Salkanpur is again an old temple of religious importance placed on the peak of the hill. It is about 75 km. South of Bhopal and about 20 km ahead of the Ratapani Wildlife Sanctuary. More than a lakh people come to visit the place during the *Navratris,* to get the blessings of the goddess. It is geologically placed at the end of the range, beyond which there is a long stretch of plains. This feature can be used for hand-gliding which is an adventure sport usually practiced in the northern States. Thus Salkanpur apart from religious tourism and cultural tourism can also provide adventure tourism to the interested tourists. Activities like hand gliding could be promoted in close coordination with some experts from Adventure clubs. As such activities would be unique in central India, these would get a lot of support from the adventure enthusiasts.

Rock climbing sites

There are several rock climbing sites in and around Bhopal. The main rock climbing sites include the rock sites near the Bull Mother Dairy Farm. The steep rock faces give rock climbers a good opportunity to test their skills. Also there are good rock faces *en route* to Ratapani near village Geeta Colony. There are also potential rock climbing sites where tourists can go and enjoy the sport. In fact the rock sites near the village Geeta colony can also be associated with the trek that is being proposed from Bhimbetka to Ginnor Fort wherein the trek could be started from Bhimbetka moving along the forest, the people who are interested could reach the Ginnor Garh fort by moving across hills doing rock climbing.

Kayaking in all major water bodies

There are number of waterbodies in and around Bhopal. Most of these waterbodies can be used for kayaking and other water sports, e.g. kayaking activities can be taken up in the river Narmada. Also kayaking can be done in the Dam sites like the Kolar Dam, Kerwa Dam and the Kaliasot Dam. These activities would create awareness among people about the adventure activities and make them more interested in these.

Findings About the Tourist

The study on the tourists was broadly carried in two categories, i.e. the Domestic Tourists and the Foreign Tourists. The study tried to find out the preferences, problems and other related aspects about the tourist. The following are the significant findings of the study.

Tourist Profile

The average age of the Domestic tourist could be approximately 35-55 years, while the average age range of the foreign tourists was 25-45 years. Most of the Domestic Tourists coming to Madhya Pradesh are from Uttar Pradesh, Gujarat, Rajasthan and Maharashtra mostly due to the adjoining borders with the State. While most of the Foreign tourists are coming from England, Germany and France.

Total tourist interviewed

Total number of tourist groups interviewed		47
I.	Domestic	31
II.	Foreign Tourist	16

Average group size

The average size of the tourist groups		7.106 (7 approx.)
I.	Domestic Tourist	9.456 (10 approx.)
II.	Foreign Tourist	2.56 (3 approx.)

Interpretation: The average size of the Indian tourist is approximately 10. The reason for this is that most of the Indian tourists move with their family or together in a group. This makes their group a large one. While the Foreign tourists move mostly in a smaller group, i.e. 2-3 people per group. The reason is that most of them come to India on a shoestring tight budget and travel alone. Generally they meet fellow tourists while travelling and then move together.

Average time to stay at a site

The average time spent at a place (days)		2.27 (2.5 approx)
I.	Domestic Tourist	1.25 (2 approx.)
II.	Foreign Tourist	2.56 (3 approx.)

Interpretation: The average time spent by Domestic tourists in a particular place is 2 days while the average time spent by the foreign tourists in a place is 3 days. The reason could be the inquisitiveness of the foreign tourists, which makes them stay in a place longer such that they are able to cover all the aspects of the place.

Willingness to pay

The average amt. willing to pay per day	291.48 (300 approx.)
I. Domestic Tourist	183.871 (190 approx.)
II. Foreign Tourist	500

Interpretation: The paying capacity of the foreign tourists is more than the Domestic tourists and hence we can see the difference.

Although the difference between what the domestic tourist wants to pay and what the foreign tourist wants to pay is not much. The reason to this is that after travelling various sites the foreign tourist also gets a fair idea as to what should be a tentative cost that they should pay and hence the difference is not very high.

Tourist preferences: The following were the results of the tourist preferences that came out of the study:

Preference for local culture

Tourists interested in the local culture	**30% (very interested), (32% interested)**
I. Domestic Tourist	18% (very interested) (33% interested)
II. Foreign Tourist	50% (very interested) (31% interested)

Preference for local cuisine

Tourists interested in the local cuisine	**26% (very interested), (30% interested)**
I. Domestic Tourist	12% (very interested) (32% interested)
II. Foreign Tourist	50% (very interested) (25% interested)

Interpretation: The domestic tourists are again not very interested in the local cuisine while the foreign tourists are very interested in the local food, although the percentage of foreigners interested in local culture to foreigners interested in local food is less because the spiciness of the Indian food which the foreigners cannot bear. But looking at the interest of the foreign tourist any ecotourism activity that is started can also have serving of Indian food as a component of the complete package.

Tourism Preferences of Different Tourists

Tourism Preferences of Domestic Tourists

Interpretation: Most of the tourism that is done in India is Religious tourism. The preference is due to the values and the customs of the Indian society. There is very little inclination of Indian tourists towards the cultural tourism, this is because the domestic tourists think that they are the part of the culture and hence they are not interested to see that. Also there is very less inclination towards the adventure tourism. This is because the people are not much aware of it and they are also not confident about the safety of the tourism. Maximum preference is definitely to the Religious tourism followed closely by Nature Tourism.

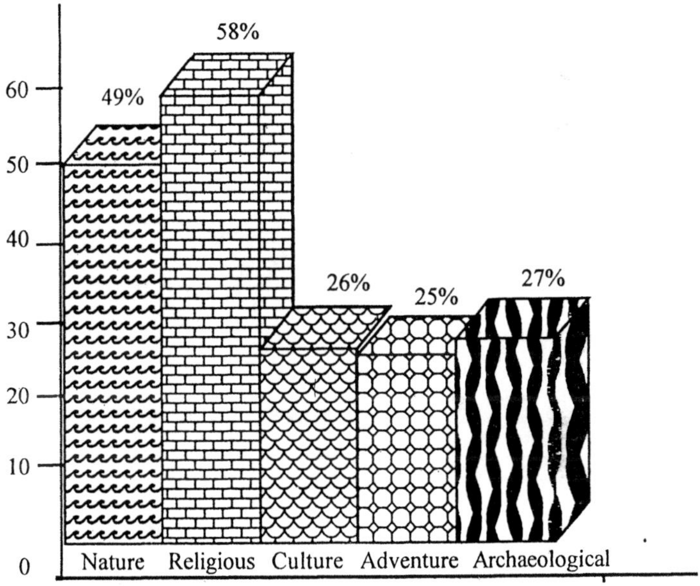

Tourism Preferences (in %)

Interpretation: The foreign tourists as shown in the graph are clearly interested in the cultural tourism. This is because they belong to a different culture and hence are more interested in the cultural diversity present in the country. This is followed by the Nature tourism and then archaeological tourism. Although foreign tourist are more interested in the adventure tourism still they do not prefer to do it in India because there are no facilities to get insured and they would not go for adventure unless they are insured.

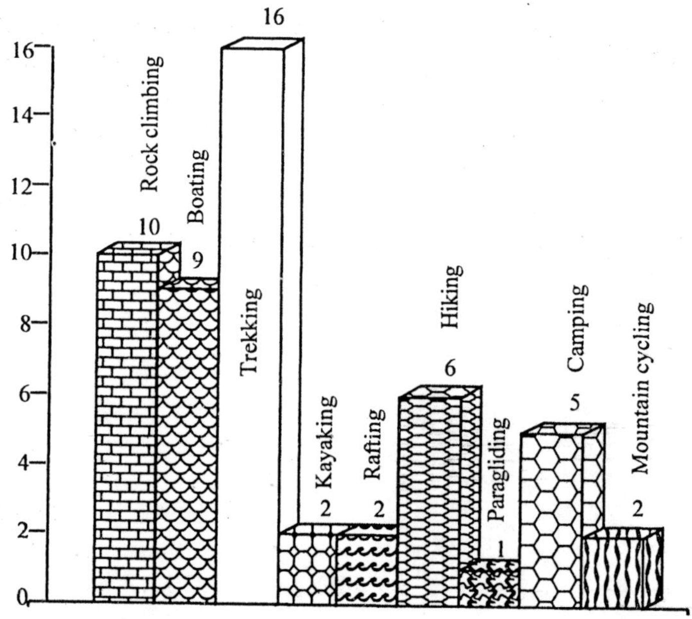

Tourist Preference of Activity

Interpretation : The following activities were given as choice to the tourist, which they would prefer. Most of the tourists were interested in trekking around the area followed by Rock Climbing. The graph clearly states that the people prefer trekking followed by Rock climbing and boating. With this information we can say that any site that has to have ecotourism potential should try to have these kinds of activities as well. These would give the tourist variety of activities to choose from. Camping and trekking go together where as Rock Climbing can be made a part of the trekking.

Major Areas of Dissatisfaction amongst Tourist

Poor Accessibility

The condition of the roads throughout the state is very bad which has lead to reduction in the arrivals of the tourist from other states. The condition is such that the tourists, who have even dared to more in the State, go back. The roads are an essential part of the Tourism in MP, as most of the tourist destinations are not connected with the Railways. Throughout the studies bad roads was the immediate complaint of the Tourists that were interviewed. There needs to be good road connections if we want to reach other tourist destinations. Many of the tourists even avoid entering the State and try to bypass the route. This reduces the inflow of the tourist to a great extent.

No Interpretation Facility

Throughout the study most of the sites that were visited lacked any kind of interpretation facility. The tourist who arrive at the site get no information as to when the site was found or what is the history of the area etc. This brings a feeling of dissatisfaction among the tourists. This is important as one of the main objectives of ecotourism is creating awareness and educating the tourists. To the question as to what all facilities the tourist want, one of the main facilities required was the development of an interpretation centre.

Pollution Around the Tourist Spots

There is a lot of pollution in and around the tourist destinations. This is a major problem for the foreign tourist. The amount of garbage littered around the site gives a very dirty feeling to the tourists that are coming to visit the site. There is a need to keep the sites clean and free to give the tourist a pleasant experience. There is very low hygiene around the tourist sites, which brings down the pleasure of visiting the site.

Costly Accommodation

The tourists find that the accommodation available at the sites is very costly. The average willingness to pay for a tourist per person per day in only Rs. 300, whereas for any tourist to get a decent room it would be difficult to get it in such an amount. The availability of Dharamshalas is also not easy. For any site to attract tourists it needs to have cheap accommodation so that people are able to spend more on the Tourist activities rather than spending just on the accommodation.

Conclusions and Recommendations

Addition of New Areas in the Circuits

Within the limited time of the study, there were a number of sites that were found which had Ecotourism Potential but which were not being made public or brought in the light.

Forest Department should play a proactive role in identifying these sites which are available in plenty throughout the state and then informing about these to the Tourism Department for its marketing at various levels like the local, national and the international level.

The identification of these sites with ecotourism potential could be done with the help of studies using systematic tools like the Ecotourism Potential Scoring etc. in consultation with the Tourist Department such that the attraction of the resources available on the site are well documented and then properly marketed.

Making New Circuits and Reorganizing Existing Circuits according to the Tourist Preferences, Time Available and the Willingness to Pay

All the present circuits available have been made on the basis of the proximity of the various tourist sites to each other, e.g. The Bhopal Circuit has got the following sites: Bhopal Lakes which has a beautiful landscape, Bhojpur which has got religious importance, Bhimbetka has archaeological importance, Sanchi again has archaeological importance, Udaigiri and Khandgiri archaeological, Ratapani WLS natural importance. All the above sites have different tourist importance. For a general tourist this is a nice circuit as it is giving various kinds of tourism opportunity in one place but the tourist who have specific preferences like Nature and Wildlife only, this circuit will not be attractive.

Hence new circuits should be made dependeing upon the tourist preferences like the Nature and Wildlife Circuit which would include all the National Parks, Wildlife Sanctuaries linked together or a Archaeological Circuit which would include all the sites with Historical importance like Mandu, Gwalior, Sanchi etc. These kinds of circuits would enhance or add value to the available sites and provides specialized packages to the tourists.

Improvement in Interpretation facilities : At present majority of sites which were visited during the study had very little or no interpretation facilities available. Forest Department should take up all the selected sites associated with it to develop interpretation centres, which would have educational programmes like slide shows, clay models of various creatures, photographs depicting various characteristics of the area etc. so that the tourist gets full information about the place and there is a rise in the satisfaction level of the tourists.

Integration of Adventure Clubs for Ecotourism Activities

In the study it was found that there is very less interaction between the Forest Department and the Adventure Clubs. In fact in the broader scene Adventure Tourism is completely missing in the State barring a few sites. The adventure clubs in the State are doing activities on their own without any knowledge and proper access to potential natural resources.

With increased coordination with the adventure clubs the Forest Department can become a facilitators by providing access to the natural resources like forests, lakes, rivers and hills where adventure activities could be performed. In turn Adventure Clubs can become the source of tourists coming in, thus mutually benefiting each other.

Better Coordination between Forest Department and the Tourism Department

It was found that there is a need to have greater interaction between the forest department and the tourism department. At most of the sites, which are associated with nature, Forest Department is trying to manage and market the site all alone. The Tourism Potential of the sites can be enhanced by greater coordination between the two departments as the Forest Department could play a key role in managing the resources while the Tourism Department could market the site well as the local, national and the international level. With better interaction between the two, there could also be training programmes organized which could help impart the skill that are available with the tourist department for delivering Tourist satisfaction to the stakeholders like the local staff, community etc. Also Tourism Department could learn more about the new places that are available inside various Parks and Sanctuaries, which have got ecotourism potential and thus be more aware of the various options available.

Indore Circuit

Rala Mandal WLS : Rala Mandal WLS is situated only 12 km South of Indore. It is a hill with average density forest. It was earlier used by the King Holkar who used to come here for hunting. The King had also built a big Hunting Lodge where they used to stay in while at their hunting trip. At present the Sanctuary has got a good number of Herbivoroes and also there are a few sightings of Panthers reported. The hunting lodge is well maintained and could be used to develop a Interpretation Centre. The proximity of the Sanctuary is also an advantage for attracting the local tourists. The Lodge could also be used for Tourist to stay there for a night or two and enjoy the natural beauty.

Dudhia Khoh : Dudhia Khoh is a waterfall situated about 30 km north-east from Indore in the Double Chowki Range. It is considered as the Dhuan Dhar of Indore. This waterfall is having a height of more than 100 feet and has got a beautiful landscape. At present there is no infrastructure available there. The waterfall is at a distance of about 35 km. from Indore. The area has got a good forest. Greenery and quietitude of the place can be harnessed for ecotourism.

Kharmor WLS : Kharmor WLS is situated only 14 km from the Agra-Bombay National Highway near Sardarpur. This sanctuary is completely on the plain grasslands. The sanctuary has got one more feature added to it, it is home to the migratory bird *Kharmor* (lesser Floricans) which comes there to breed and grow there young ones. Since the sanctuary is very near to the highway hence its accessibility is good and people can come and stay there for a night or two and enjoy the beautiful landscape that the plain grassland offers. An Interpretation centre can also be developed to educate the tourist coming for sighting the Floricans.

Bagh Caves (Buddhist Sites) : Bagh Caves are situated near the town Bagh that is about 50 km from Dhar. These caves have been carved inside the hill. Tehre are seven caves out of which three caves have big Stupa's built inside the caves. There are beautiful paintings done inside the caves, which date back to sixth, seventh century. The Archaelogical Survey of India has also developed a Museum where infromation about the paintings and various sculptures are kept the caves are situated just adjacent to the Bagh River, which flows for most of the months. The Bagh Caves can be considered equivalent to the Udaigiri and Khandgiri caves.

Katthiwada (proposed WLS) : Katthiwada is a tribal dominated area, which is situated 90 km from Jhabua. It forms the border of Gujarat and Madhya Pradesh. The area is a hilly area covered with dense forest. The forest density in the open areas in reported to be .6 and in the closed areas the density is about .8, which indicates a very good forest. The area has got beautiful climate even in the dry season due to the forest. The hills along with the forest give a very beautiful Landscape. Katthiwada has also got a proposal for the sloth bear sanctuary. All these factors make Katthiwada a good destination for the nature tourist. Trekking inside the dense jungle and reaching the highest points in the Katthiwada region can be a great experience for the nature lovers. The tribal culture associated with Katthiwada is also unique and the foreigners do come to visit the place to see the culture of the tribes during the month of March and April when the melas are organized.

Alirajpur : Alirajpur situated in Jhabua district is also known for the tribal culture and there melas. There are people coming from all around the world to see the unique culture and the various activities that are happening during the mela season which is the month of March or April. Although the area is a bit far from the highways but it becomes a experience worth moving to the place.

Omkareshwar-Maheshwar Kayaking : Omkareshwar is situated at the banks of the river Narmada. It is a beautiful site to see. The river further moves around 30 km to reach Maheshwar. The course of the river throughout is very light. There can be kayaking started where people can row there kayaks from Omkareshwar to Maheshwar and in between stop at various places to have snacks etc. this can give boost to the local trade as well. After reaching Maheshwar the tourists can visit the Devi Ahilya Bai's Palace. Thus this kind of kayaking would be unique and could provide an enriching experience in which the tourist has a adventure experience followed by a visit to a historical monument.

Wanchu Point : Wanchu point is the highest point in the Manpur Range situated 50 km south of Indore. The point is known because it is used to store water that is brought from Narmada to a height so that it could be supplied to Indore by the gravitational force. The point is at a height and after this there are plain lands for more than 15 km. In the night Wanchu point gives a unique experience. This is because in the night the lights of all the villages below could be seen which give the impression as if all the stars have come below and we are standing above the stars. Moreover the landscape during the sunrise and the sunset is beautiful. The point is frequently visited by the local tourists.

Kheoni WLS : Kheoni Wildlife Sanctuary is about 90 km from Indore and Bhopal. The sanctuary in the earlier time was used as a game park provided by the Holkar King to the local population. It comes under the Dewas division. The sanctuary has got a good dense forest. There is good herbivorous population. The sanctuary has got a lot of area, which has got hilly terrain this area could be used for the trekking purpose. The sanctuary has got a rest house where tourist can come and enjoy the nature.

13

LANDSCAPE BASED ECOTOURISM PLANNING

EXPLORING ECOTOURISM POTENTIAL OF SEONI DISTRICT

A.K. Bhattacharya, B.M.S. Rathore, Kumar Rahul and Sanjay Bala

Madhya Pradesh has announced State Biodiversity Strategy and Action Plan 2002, which underlines the need of ecodevelopment in the State to conserve its biodiversity heritage. The Government of Madhya Pradesh had also announced its new Eco and Adventure Tourism Policy (2001-02). These policy initiatives provide a consistent framework to explore possibilities in the ecotourism sector, a new *mantra* in travel and tourism. The ecotourism has recently become very important for the areas having rich cultural and biological heritage.

The Satpura uplands have great diversity and richness of cultural and biological heritage. Seoni being a part of this region also has its share of these endowments. Pench is the most visible and renowned testimony of such natural endowments. Many other potential ecotourism sites are considerably underutilized for want of awareness, infrastructure and facilities, and lack of innovation in development of ecotourism products and packages. In spite of that the current aggregated tourist turnover of different sites included in this study has been estimated to around 60,000 to 70,000 per annum. It has also been estimated that more than 70 per cent of these visitors come from an area within a radius of 50 km from the sites.

During the study it was discovered that some sites which are relatively non-descript at present has high ecotourism potential in terms of their intrinsic values for recreation, education, and adventure. The sites like Shikara-Payili was found to be quite comparable to its better known cousin Pench on ecotourism potential score defined in the study.

The present benefit to the local community is rather limited. They are mainly in terms of income from putting up a stall during *melas* (fares) and employment in tourism based activities at relatively recognized sites like Pench. But this is only a tip of the iceberg. The potential benefits to local community are enormous in terms of increased income/employment, and market outreach to local products and services. To harness such benefits, public investments are required along with capability building of local community in terms of training and education to enable them to make most of the emerging opportunities inherent in the ecotourism sector.

The study also tried to capture the present profile of tourists who come to visit Pachmarhi. It was found that a large number of tourists are well educated and affluent. Waterbodies and hills are the most preferred choices in features/attributes of an ecotourism destination. An overwhelming majority of tourists (64%) visit a site/destination for recreation/relaxation.

A strategy to realize ecotourism potential of Seoni should primarily consist of development of ecotourism resources, innovative ecotourism products and packages and promotion of potential ecotourism sites/destinations through media. A collaboration and partnership between different government departments is required to improve the basic infrastructure like roads and communication. An alliance between private sector and local communities need to be fostered to improve facilities/services required by tourists and to ensure that the communities get a fair share in the benefits.

About the Study

Objectives

- Ecotourism resource inventory of Seoni.
- Understanding ecotourism market.

- Suggest a broad strategy for developing ecotourism prospects of Seoni.

Scope of the Study

The study is exploratory in nature. The study uses primarily qualitative approach in its methodology.

Although the geographical area covered for the study was Seoni-Chhindwara-Pachmarhi stretch of Satpura uplands, the focus of the study was Seoni district with a clear direction to explore potential and opportunities for the district for benefit of people especially local community.

An Indicative Strategy

I. Preparing a Development Strategy for Seoni District: A framework :

Goals

- Conserve biological (and cultural) heritage and promote their sustainable use by generating income, jobs and business opportunities in ecotourism and related business for benefit of local community.

Objectives

- Education and awareness about cultural and natural heritage.
- Economic incentive to local community to be willing partner in conservation.
- Enhance local business and employment opportunities and market outreach of local products.
- Decrease dependence on forest.

Guiding principles

- The sustainability of ecotourism from the environmental, economic and socio-cultural points of view.
- Involvement and empowerment of local communities and indigenous people in the ecotourism development process, in

management and monitoring of ecotourism activities, and in the sharing of benefits resulting from it.

Recommended approach: Major elements of the strategy

1. Ecotourism Resource Developments

Prioritizing the sites

10 ecotourism sites selected on the basis of their performance on ecotourism potential score are given in Table 13.1. It is recommended that the following table should be taken into account to prioritize from among different ectourism potential sites.

Table 13.1 : List of ten sites having highest ecotourism potential in Seoni

Sl. No.	*Ecotourism Sites/Resources*	*EP score*
1	Pench National Park	3.00
2	Shikra-Payili	2.46
3	Ghoghraghat	2.35
4	Siddhghat	2.32
5	Hatidoh	2.25
6	Nanhikanar	2.22
7	Rani Durgawati Fort	2.06
8	Kuraigarh	2.00
9	Ambamai (Nanhikanar)	1.99
10	Parewa Khoh	1.96

Site specific ecotourism plans

Site specific ecotourism plans should be formulated jointly with consultation of all stakeholders. Economic and ecological feasibility study should precede any large and long term investment.

2. Infrastructure, Facilities and Services

Infrastructure, facilities and services at most of the sites are either in poor shape or non-existent. It is very important that the following basic needs should be met to improve ecotourism profile of Seoni.

- Roads and transport

- Food and accommodation
- Simple facilities like benches, sheds at the site

Committing adequate financial and other resources

Public investment is needed to boost ecotourism values of a potential site. The necessary resources should be mobilized by interdepartmental arrangement to provide infrastructure, such as access roads and assist local community in providing tourism services and facilities at the site to enhance its ecotourism potential. A district fund should be created from collaboration with different departments and donations from national and international donor agencies for investment in improving infrastructure of the sites which would then multiply the volumes of tourists visiting these sites form of various types of assistance.

Private sector businesses should be encouraged to invest for development of different sites. The government should act as facilitator in strengthening the links of these businesses with local communities.

Collaboration and partnership

For successful harnessing of ecotourism potential a strategic partnership between different government departments and agencies is required. A collaboration between different stakeholders also need to be fostered which should include, but does not limit itself to, private investors/entrepreneurs, local communities, civil society organizations.

Promotion

Almost all of the sites need promotion. To promote these sites the following measures would be of great value :

- Incentives to tour operators and travel agencies.
- Internet for extended outreach in the premium segment.
- Campaign with print and electronic media which should include sponsored visits to ecotourism potential sites by reporters, photographers and other resource persons from media
    - Signboards,
    - Cultural festivals.

3. Developing Ecotourism Products and Packages

Ecotourism products and packages should be designed keeping in view the well recognized ecotourism sites and routes. The possible ecotourism products can be broadly classified into five categories:

- Group package
- Affinity package
- Family package
- Soft adventure
- Nature and wildlife

List of Recommended Ecotourism Products for Seoni

Group package :

Educational tours

- Demystifying herbs for people
- Field trips for school and colleges
- Arts festivals
- Summer camp
- Railway voyage (narrow gauge)

Affinity package

- Arts workshops
- Photography
- Yoga and spirituality

Family package

- Honeymoon/intimate getaway
- Island vacation
- Fishing
- Health and fitness

Nature and wildlife

- Jungle expedition
- Safari
- Camping
- Wildlife viewing

Adventure

- Canoeing / kayaking
- Caravan / convoy tours
- Hiking and Trekking
- Rock climbing

Community participation

The effective involvement of the local communities in Ecotourism will require the following interventions :

Capacity Building

Training programmes for local people and enterprises and other stakeholders would encourage their meaningful participation in adopting a new mode of livelihood from ecotourism. The communities may be trained in making handicrafts, as well as managerial and business skills required for small enterprise. Such capacity building, especially of youth will have a key influence on positive future directions of ecotourism for local economy.

Microcredit to Established Ecotourism based Enterprises

Easily accessible micro-credit and other assistance should be provided to small, medium and micro-enterprises which should be well targetted. This will enable local community to make necessary investment in providing services and facilities to the tourists. Some of the basic facilities which can very economically be made available to tourists include accommodation and food during village stay. Villagers should be encouraged to erect a few huts in the village where tourists might stay.

Educating community

Awareness through educational and extension programmes about ecotourism opportunities in local customs, cuisine, festivals, arts and crafts will be instrumental in increasing overall attractiveness of the sites and supporting entrepreneurship among local community. The community should also be educated about conservation of biodiversity at ecotourism potential sites.

Facilitating Linkages and the Networking

The government should encourage strategic alliances between private business and local community. The community should also be encouraged to enter into co-operative ecotourism ventures to take advantage of synergy and economy of scale. In the design of different ecotourism products, specially those which focus on entertainment, ethnic component of dance, music might be an attraction in itself. As local community might lack the necessary sophistication in marketing and organize a cultural extravaganza, a linkage between private entrepreneurs and local community need to be fostered. This will not only increase the benefits which the community will have from ecotourism but will also enhance the attraction of site/destination to the tourists.

Ensuring Benefits

Any development of services/facilities should be designed and managed in such a way that income generated from them is retained in local economy and the local community gets maximum benefit out of them.

Institutional Frameworks

Local institutions like *Gram Panchayat,* Forest Protection Committee should be involved in any initiative to develop ecotourism so that the community feel a sense of ownership and put into its strengths and resources for the success of such initiatives. Such institutional framework will act as an interface between community and other stakeholders of the ecotourism sector. These institutions have potential to work as regulatory mechanism to encourage good ecotourism practices and standards. The present system of involving ecodevelopment committee in different ecotourism activities within a protected area should be continued.

14

ECOTOURISM AND LIVELIHOOD

A CASE STUDY FROM BANDHAVGARH NATIONAL PARK

A.K. Bhattacharya and Sudipto Ghosh

Since the Earth Summit held in Rio de Janeiro in 1992, pressure has grown for the tourism industry to lift its environmental performance in common with other economic sectors, and to work towards ecologically sustainable forms of tourism development. At the same time, planners and developers seeking to create satisfying settings for the tourists into the next century must anticipate a world influenced by a new bewildering array of forces, many of which are difficult to predict. Given such uncertainty, the challenge is to pursue tourism growth in a manner resilient enough to respond positively to a changing global environment and societal structure, while remaining compatible with the principles and practice of ecologically sustainable development (Tourism, Development and Growth, 1997)

The tourism industry in the current years is looking for sustainable development. The industry needs to carry on profitably despite all the shocks of the modern world. And it also needs to develop future tourists with the interest to visit the tourism places rich with diversity. For the tourism sector, the concept of sustainability implies meeting current uses and demands of tourism without impairing the natural and cultural heritage, or opportunities for collective enjoyment of tourists of the future (Hawkes and Williams, 1993).

As an attraction to mass tourism, which has caused negative social, economical and ecological impacts, ecotourism is the latest product the tourism industry is trying to project. It is a focused journey to natural areas to understand the history of environment, without altering the genuineness of the ecosystem, while producing economic opportunities that make conservation of natural resources beneficial to the local people. If it does not satisfy anyone of these conditions then it cannot be called a real ecotourism programme (*Tourism India,* 2002).

The main problem of the tourism industry in the recent years is the uncontrolled growth of tourist inflow in some of the destination sites. And also to attract the tourist and to delve into a good business opportunity newer sites with high potential to attract the tourists are being located and developed.

Bandhavgarh Tiger Reserve (BTR) has taken a definitive step towards community-based ecotourism. Nature based tourism is currently being conducted at BTR. A part of the community is getting benefits from present nature of tourism.

In community-based ecotourism, the maximum benefits should go to the local community. BTR authority is trying to achieve ecotourism within its current jurisdiction and with its limited natural resources it trying to provide the maximum benefit to the community.

The authority has already taken the first step in this matter. They are now willing to know the state of tourism and the amount of benefits that are flowing to the community through tourism. After the understanding of the current nature and the practices involved with tourism it is needed to plan for the future. While planning it is also necessary to develop necessary criteria and indicators to manage and monitor the growth.

The overall objectives of the project were :

- To assess the tangible and intangible economic values of ecotourism in BTR.
- To determine the economic contribution of the ecotourism to the different stakeholders.
- To examine the potential of ecotourism in the light of sustainable livelihoods of the local communities and other stakeholders.

- To evolve verifiable indicators for ecotourism.

Standard methodology was used in the study. The methodology include

- Collection of primary and secondary data.
- Field-survey of socio-economic, visitation and ecological parameters.
- Focused group discussion with the stakeholders.
- Analysis of data collected to examine the impact of Ecotourism in BTR.

The degree of local participation is often limited not only in terms of ownership and control, but also in terms of enjoyment of the natural attraction (Ecotourism: a sustainable option, 1993). Ecotourism tries to increase this participation upto the level of actual management of the natural resources by the local people.

After studying all the components of ecotourism at BTR it was found that at Bandhavgarh though currently nature based tourism is going on there is need to develop several components to attain ecotourism. And above all ecotourism then can be used as a management tool to attain welfare for the local people and *vice versa.*

Some of the activities need to be undertaken as prerequisite for ecotourism :

- Capacity building of the EDCs.
- Capacity building of the guides and staffs of the forest department for efficient handling of the tourists.
- The villagers should be provided with micro-credit for running small scale income generating activities.
- People should be encouraged to reduce the pressure on the forest.
- And above all a master plan should be formed for the BTR by the FD with all other acting government departments in this region for the betterment of the local people.

The findings of the study and the recommendations urge the

best possible efforts of the Forest Department at Bandhavgarh to use ecotourism as a management tool for the betterment of the local people of BTR.

Recommendations

Capacity Building of Eco-Development Committees (EDCs)

There are 78 villages in and around BTR. Only 46 villages are having EDCs formed.

The goal of 'Eco-development' in BTR is to conserve all natural ecosystems within BTR by keeping the 'core area' fully intact and meeting all public requirements from the 'Buffer zone'.

The objectives of EDCs are:

1. to reduce dependency of the local people on the PA;
2. to minimize man-animal conflict; and
3. to win support of the local people for conservation.

Currently in most of the EDCs, the number of members, who are regularly attending the meetings, is very few. Also due to this the works of the EDCs are not having any effect to the life of the local people. By and large it can be found that the EDCs somehow only exist without any function.

Strengths

Already 46 EDCs have been formed and people are registered with these committees. Also the FD staffs are in place in the committees and they are aware with the proceedings of the EDC.

Weaknesses

There are another 31 villages where EDCs are not present. Also the members of the currently existing committees are not satisfied with the proceedings of the committees. Most of the people are not aware of the rules and regulations of the EDC and most of the EDCs are non-functional or redundant on their current state of function.

Proposed Action

EDCs should be formed in all the villages. And then there is need for capacity building of the staff member in-charge and the local members. For these there is need to provide training to them on various issues. There should be training components on:

1. Educating the members about the policies and planning process by which EDCs are governed.
2. The current practice of patrolling by the committee members should be controlled and wireless sets should be provided to each EDC for effective communication with the FD Staff.
3. Trainings for other income generating activities should be imparted to the villagers on the basis of demand and payment. The fee to be charged should be only for sustaining the training project. The training for making handicrafts and souvenirs can be given from local experts and training for tailoring and repairing electronic goods can be provided by bringing experts from outside BTR.

Support should be given to the people engaged in making of handicrafts and performing dances and other stage performance. Suitable market for these kinds of products and performance should be explored and promoted.

Also encouragement should be given by FD the people about:

1. Protection of the forest.
2. Stall feeding of the livestock and whenever possible buying high milk producing cows and buffaloes.
3. Building of Biogas plants for those people having sufficient amount of livestock to support the running of a Biogas plant.

Capacity building of the guides and staff of the forest department for efficient handling of the tourists with increase in infrastructure

Tourist is the heart of the ecotourism function as without the presence of tourist there cannot be anything called ecotourism.The guides and the most of the staff of the FD working at BTR are not equipped enough to handle the tourists. The Interpretation Centre, the Internet Café and the Museum are currently in non-functional state. All these facilities should be running with full vigour to cater effectively to the tourists.

Strengths

Adequate number of guides and staff are present at the disposal of the FD. And most of these persons have enough knowledge about BTR, specially in case of guides all of the people are given registration after a tough examination, about the knowledge of BTR and specially about flora and fauna.

The buildings of the Interpretation Centre, the Internet Café and the Museum are currently in good state. Also computers are present in the Interpretation Centre.

Weakness

Most of these people within the guides and the FD are not able to communicate in English and that becomes a major hurdle to communicate with most of the tourists coming from different parts of the country and the rest of the world. The Interpretation Centre, the Internet Café and the Museum are currently in non-functional state due to lack of staff.

Proposed Action

The facilities for the tourists, to achieve tourist satisfaction, should be running and the people should be from local origin. The following facilities should be strengthened :

1. An interpretation centre should be running for the tourists to let them quench their thirst of knowledge about the area. Four local graduates should be engaged with sufficient knowledge of spoken English so that they can interact with the tourists of all over the world.
2. The Internet Café should be started immediately with two local graduates with a little knowledge of computer

operation. They could be made proficient with short-term training courses. They should also be able to talk and understand English for proper interaction with the tourists.

3. The museum should be developed with proper facilities and persons to guide the tourists. There should be two Graduates with sufficient knowledge of English. Also with them two other local literate persons should be engaged for the maintenance of the museum.
4. All the guides, FD staffs and the local gypsy-drivers should be given training about the rules and regulations governing the Tiger Reserve. And a coaching class on spoken English should be started for these people. The coaching class should be on a payment basis.

Increasing Agricultural Productivity and Starting of Agro-Forestry to Reduce Dependency of the Local People on Forest

Agriculture is the major source of livelihood for the local people. Most of the people have small landholdings or a large amount of land divided into many fragments. The major problem in this area is crop damages by wild animals and at most of the places there is no irrigation facility available. Even if water is present for irrigation but the crop damage by wild animals reduces the level of production by 50 per cent of the original productivity of the land. Also there is no agro-forestry practice available in this region.

Strengths

Fertile agricultural lands are available to the local farmers. Also adequate rainfall is present in the area to support agriculture. BTR is also having a perennial water source in form of a river, Charan Ganga.

Weaknesses

A lot of the agricultural fields are devoid of any irrigational facilities. Also crop damages by wild animals is a major problem in this area.

And most of the people are holding fragmented lands for agriculture. Due to unavailability of water for irrigation and crop damage by wild animals most of the people are doing agricultural activities only in bigger fields that are near to water source.

Proposed Action

Since agriculture is the major source of livelihood so it is expected that by increasing the productivity of the agricultural fields from the current state would reduce the dependency of the people of forest thus reducing the pressure on the forest. The requirements for this are:

1. Encouraging the people to take loans from the EDC and do proper fencing of the agricultural crops. The loans should be returned within a time period of five years.
2. Creation of a number of stop dams in each village and providing them with pumps for the purpose of irrigation. Also one person in each village should be appointed to look after these facilities by paying a token amount of money by collecting the same from the villagers for using the service.
3. Also a nursery should be developed by FD to develop seedlings of plants like Harra, Haldu and Aonla, with a number of locally available medicinal plants. Two local people could be engaged to look after these facilities and the seedlings should be distributed at a minimum cost. For the production of medicinal plants the crop after harvest could be collected from the villagers and then sold to the market through the EDCs.

Ecotourism Promotion Activities

BTR should be promoted as a major ecotourism centre. For these there is need to do certain things and in this direction help from other existing Departments like Tourism, Zila Panchayat etc. can be taken, whenever necessary.

Strengths

BTR is already known to the world as a tourist spot with wildlife attraction. The highest density of the tiger at BTR attracts a lot of people as tourists, both national and international.

Weakness

No promotional activities are present from the FD to attract more tourists. There should be very good quality brochures about BTR and its tourism assets are available for the tourists.

Proposed Action

The necessary steps for promotion are as follows :

1. Proper documentation of BTR is needed. The documentation should also be available in the market for other persons to buy.
2. Restrictions on the use of polythene bags should be imposed. Also there is need of installation of dustbins in and around the tourism entry points and if possible set up of public urinals.
3. Creation of attractive and new brochures about Bandhavgarh Tiger Reserve, the historical places within the jungle, animals, birds, trees and butterflies.
4. Creation of new packages to attract different interest groups like scientific excursions.

Regulating Tourist and Vehicle Inflow

The area of tourism zone of BTR is only 110 sq. km. approximately. Being small region there is need to control the number of vehicles that can be allowed to enter inside the park.

Strengths

Already there are number of people diploid through FD for tourism. They can be used as regulatory persons.

Weakness

No rules are available to control the number of tourists and the vehicles that can enter the Park for enjoying the resources.

Proposed Action

There is need to:

1. Conduct a study to know the carrying capacity of the tourism zone.
2. Increase the tourism zone to accommodate the anticipated increase in the number of tourists

Strengthening Protection Activities

The path towards the community-based ecotourism does not mean there is no need to strengthen the protection of the Park. The protection is needed for proper maintenance of habitat and to stop any kind of poaching activities.

Without strong protection the tiger population and its habitat is going to decrease under the increasing pressure of population and its demand for wood and other exotic and rare mementos.

Strengths

Already a large number of personnel are deployed by the FD to protect the Park with a number of wireless sets for connectivity. Also a large number of vehicles are at the disposal of the FD for quick reach to any place of disturbance.

Weakness

At many places within the forest, people from outside can still enter without the notice of the FD.

Proposed Action

The current need is of more wireless sets for the forest guards and labours in charge of protecting the forest. Also there is need to quick resolution of the court cases against the miscreants with stronger punishment. For this there is a need to influence the policy on forest protection act and building up special courts whenever possible. Without a proper political will there is very little chance to influence the policy for the good of BTR and other similar PAs.

Proposed Action for Influencing Policy in Favour of Ecotourism

The policy on tourism within the PAs should be influenced so that a large area could be opened for the tourists. It should be considered that the increasing number of tourists should also be accommodated. But while opening a large amount of area for the tourists one should not forget to maintain the quality of the forest. For this, periodic opening and closing of areas within the PA could be done, such that the nature can heal itself during the time of closure. Applying this same principle the Park can be opened for all round the year. This will not only help the current available forms of business to run successfully all through the year but will also create greater number of mandays of job for the local people.

Other Necessary Actions

There are also some other issues, which has to be addressed while travelling towards a brighter future. The issues are:

1. One proper market should be created for the local people where the lodges and resorts can buy foodgrains, vegetables and other local produce for the guests in their place. This in turn would increase the demand for the local produce.
2. The vehicles running inside the Park with the tourists should be registered with the FD and only those vehicles with proper registration should be allowed inside the Park. This will increase the chance of the local vehicle owners and the drivers to achieve more gain. If possible the rate for a vehicle to enter with tourist for a single day should be fixed and a roster system could be developed for these vehicles to get a chance to enter the Park.
3. Proper signboards should be displayed to guide the tourists in different areas both inside the forest campus and in those areas where the tourists concentration outside the forest is must, e.g. Tala.
4. Proper system should be developed to get feedback both from the tourists and other stakeholders. All these

feedbacks should be analyzed from time to time and necessary actions should be taken.

5. Tourists should be encouraged to visit Bandhavgarh more and more. For this, code numbers could be assigned to each tourist and 10 per cent to 20 per cent of fee could be wavered for a tourist if he/she visits BTR again within a span of two years. With the increase of repeated visits there will be more number of tourists visiting at BNP, increasing the demand for the local goods and services. Thus in turn it will increase the income of the local people.
6. A master plan for BTR should be prepared with other government departments working at Bandhavgarh for the betterment of the local people. The need of the master plan is to ensure that there should not be any repetition in the development works and thus greater number of people could be benefited.

INDEX